Unsung Heroes of Old Japan

JAPAN LIBRARY

Unsung Heroes of Old Japan

Michifumi Isoda

Translated by
Juliet Winters Carpenter

Japan Publishing Industry Foundation for Culture

Note on conventions used
Dates are given according to the Western (Gregorian) calendar.
In general, Japanese names appearing in this book are given in Japanese order, family name first, except for the author's name, which follows the Western order.

Michifumi Isoda
Unsung Heroes of Old Japan
Translated by Juliet Winters Carpenter

Published by Japan Publishing Industry Foundation for Culture (JPIC),
3-12-3 Kanda-Jinbocho, Chiyoda-ku, Tokyo 101-0051, Japan

First edition: March 2017

© Michifumi Isoda, 2012
English translation copyright © 2017 by Japan Publishing Industry Foundation for Culture.

Originally published in Japanese under the title of *Mushi no nihonjin*, by Bungeishunju Ltd. in 2012.

English language rights arranged with Bungeishunju Ltd.

Jacket and cover design by Point & Line Co., Ltd.
Jacket and cover illustration: Street scene of Honchō, from *Edo meisho zue* (National Diet Library)

As this book is published primarily to be donated to overseas universities, research institutions, public libraries and other organizations, commercial publication rights are available. For all enquiries regarding those rights, please contact the publisher of the original Japanese edition at the following address: foreignrights@bunshun.co.jp

All rights reserved. Printed in Japan.
ISBN 978-4-916055-76-7
http://www.jpic.or.jp/japanlibrary/

Preface to the English edition

I have waited eagerly for the day when *Unsung Heroes of Old Japan* would be translated into English and made available to people around the world. I wrote the book with the faint hope that people might one day become more like the men and women portrayed here. Whether humanity has any universal values, I can't say. But looking back over the sweep of human history, I am convinced that values like those shown here result in happiness for the individual and society.

The world is about to enter on an age ruled by the value of "me first"—an age when people pursue self-interest above all else, without a thought for others. But history teaches us that the blind pursuit of self-interest is in no one's best interest. Perhaps a Robinson Crusoe living alone on a desert island could get by with thinking only of what benefits him, but the world is so small and contains so many others that matters grow complicated. Acting always in one's own interest makes one's own interest unsustainable.

In this book, I have written of a time some 150 to 300 years ago when samurai, the warrior class, made up five percent of the population of Japan. In all there were approximately 30 million people. The land was at peace, with all arable land under cultivation. The samurai, having no more wars to fight, became bureaucrats responsible for enforcing a strict legal code. Farmers gave forty percent of their crops to samurai as land tax. To preserve their livelihood, they worked hard and studied hard, too. Adult literacy among both sexes was around forty percent, below comparable rates in England, Germany, and France, but higher than in Italy. Many Japanese farmers had an intellectual bent. They were among the first in the world to develop a market economy.

Some farmers and common people in this premodern society developed a natural, penetrating awareness. I have written about them in the pages of this book. Japanese society in those days was built on class discrimination, with highest respect given to feudal lords, the top-ranking members of the samurai class. All samurai were entitled to ride on horseback or in a palanquin. But those who ride horses cause suffering to their mounts, and those who ride in palanquins cause suffering to their bearers. The people truly deserving of respect are those who set out to cause no suffering to any other living being. Ordinary farmers reached this level of awareness and used their wits to conduct legal and economic negotiations with the ruling samurai to construct a system under which all might live in happiness.

People should live in mutual sympathy, without distinction between self and others. Their worth should be judged not by how much they have accumulated but by how much they have given. I have written here about a number of Japanese people who believed these things and lived by their beliefs. Today when class, race, and nationality threaten to divide us, I challenge the world to live up to the spirit of these men and women of long ago.

Michifumi Isoda
Kyoto, 2017

Contents

1. Kokudaya Jūzaburō
(1719–1777)

Spring comes late in the northern province of Michinoku, but no sooner do the fields turn green with new shoots, and cherry trees burst into bud, than all at once the peach trees blossom and the hills come vibrantly alive. Fresh water springs up as if a dam had burst, rippling into the rice paddies and refreshing the villages. Never was there any more glorious spring than the spring in Michinoku that day in 1766.

And yet for some time now Jūzaburō had been downcast, trudging through the post town. This station on the Ōshū Kaidō, the highway connecting Michinoku with the far-off capital of Edo, was called Yoshioka. It consisted of some two hundred households. Just outside the town was a milepost, and above it a great cedar soared high as if defying the heavens. The Yoshioka milepost was sixth from the castle town, so Sendai was only six miles away; but the residents of Yoshioka, nearly all of them part-time farmers, were exceedingly poor.

Beyond the row of shabby thatched-roof houses was a range of hills called Nanatsumori—Seven Forests—as picturesque as any scenery painted on a six-fold screen. Ever since he was a boy, Jūzaburō had loved this view and gazed at it with pleasure morning and night. But the more beautiful the spring weather today, the heavier a weight seemed to descend on him, robbing him of any inclination to enjoy the scenery. He felt a deep, helpless exasperation.

As Jūzaburō walked glumly along, letting his feet take him where they would, he passed entirely through the little town and soon found himself standing before Sekijō-sama, a small shrine on the bank of the Yoshida River. Long ago the townspeople had made a dike there to divert water for their paddies. In springtime, horsetails grew along the riverbank near the shrine, and when he was a boy, Jūzaburō often used to come and pick them. But when he told the grownups where he had got them, they would fall silent. He thought this was strange, and one day he asked his father about it.

"We have to be grateful for Sekijō-sama," his father said. "The Yoshida looks peaceful, but from ancient times, whenever there was a big flood, the dike would burst. Everyone talked it over, and they decided to make a human sacrifice. I don't know where the victim was from. I heard that over in Ōhira they seized an itinerant *miko*"—shamanic medium—"who fell to the ground and begged for her life, but they shut their ears, bound her, and buried her alive. The shrine they built to honor her is called Miko Gozensha. You've seen it, haven't you? Well, something just that cruel may have happened here in Yoshioka. In any case, that's how we've avoided floods, and how we've been blessed with plenty of water for the paddies, too."

Shocked, Jūzaburō hoped the story wasn't true. He raised pleading eyes to his father.

"It's no lie," his father said. "One year the dike broke and human bones appeared. One of the village elders said they were the bones of the sacrificial victim and they should be enshrined."

That was the origin of Sekijō-sama. The shrine faced east so that it could overlook the paddies as they were flooded and later as ripe ears waved in the breeze, heavy with grain. A dull light had shone in his father's eyes as he talked, as if he himself might be made a human sacrifice.

His father, Asanoya Jinnai VI, had been dead now for three years. He'd been head of the most influential merchant family in Yoshioka. The family had brewed sake for generations, but his father had been drawn less to the life of trade than to the life of learning. He used to take pleasure in gathering the local children and teaching them to read and write for free, as if he were running a small private school.

Jūzaburō was the eldest son, born when his father was twenty. Yet rather than taking over the family business as the first son should do, he'd been adopted into the Kokudaya family—owners of a neighboring sake brewery who lacked an heir. Jūzaburō's father, being on close terms with them, had suggested to Jūzaburō that he step in, which he had done. Objections were raised—"Surely there's no need to give up the firstborn son"—but somehow that was what happened. Now the head of the family, Asanoya Jinnai VII, was Jūzaburō's younger brother, four years his junior. Sometimes it seemed to Jūzaburō that his father had turned his back on him, abandoned him—but there was no point in dwelling on such things now.

What he remembered best about his father was how, late in life, he would speak often of "perpetual prosperity," as if consumed with the idea. At first, Jūzaburō hadn't really understood what he meant.

"We have to see to it that everyone in Yoshioka can make a go of it," his father would sometimes say. "Before I die, I want to do something to ensure that the town can enjoy perpetual prosperity." These were not empty words. His eyes were sad, and he spoke from the heart. In his later years he'd been so melancholy that when he died the priest at the local temple gave him the posthumous Buddhist name Kyōun'an Daiyomukei. The first part, literally "education chance," was appropriate for someone whose hobby had been teaching children, but the second part meant "great honor, no joy."

Only recently had Jūzaburō gained a dim understanding of what had so concerned his father. Just the other day, he'd said to himself, "Yoshioka is getting to be dreadfully poor. What will become of it?" A surge of alarm swept through him. Abandoned houses lined the main street of this town where he was born and grew up, interspersed with weed-grown empty lots like gaps in the teeth of a comb. At this rate the town would soon fall so deeply into poverty that no escape would be possible. His father, a man of vision, had seen the end coming.

Asanoya was by far the most prosperous establishment in the post town, and Kokudaya also had a sizable fortune. Both Jūzaburō's own family and his adopted family would survive. If he thought only about the welfare of those two families, there was nothing to worry about, but the prospect of friends and neighbors slowly succumbing to starvation was horrifying. Imagining the future of Yoshioka filled him with fear. Did the shogunate—the shogun's central administration—exist to wipe out farmers? Jūzaburō had been driven to wonder this. That was why he was so dejected. When the authorities no longer protected people's livelihood, what recourse did the people have? He mulled this question over as he walked along.

If only Yoshioka were under the daimyo's direct control! But no, the daimyo had bestowed this land on a vassal of his. That was the origin of all their trouble. Yoshioka had been granted to a vassal in the Tadaki family with a stipend of 1,500 koku. He wasn't incompetent, but 1,500 koku wasn't enough for the lord of a fief. He couldn't properly provide for or look after his people. The residents of Yoshioka smoldered with resentment. It was unfair that they alone should have to suffer this way.

Jūzaburō had begun to think that no daimyo was as old-fashioned as Lord Date Shigemura (1742–1796) of Sendai. The Date clan was of ancient lineage, descended from an immediate vassal of the shogun back in the twelfth century. Having long held sway in this northern hinterland, they used ancient practices to an almost unbelievable degree. To measure land, for example, rather than the widespread system based on the yield of rice, Sendai still used a coin-based system that was a relic from the fifteenth century. One kammon, a string of one hundred coins, represented about two acres of land; so what other provinces would call a "ten-koku fief," the Date clan referred to as a "ten-kammon fief." Sendai farmers followed suit, measuring off their land in kammon.

The Date clan didn't require its principal retainers to reside permanently in the castle town. They were scattered across the vast territory of the domain. Some were given residences in the castle town and made to spend alternate years there, just as daimyo were required to do in the capital of Edo. This sort of arrangement was unusual, and the resulting processions made a bizarre spectacle.

After the 1615 defeat of the Toyotomi clan establishing the Tokugawa regime, a decree went out: "one province, one castle." Daimyo were prohibited from building a large number of citadels. The Date clan, however, had managed to get around this prohibition. Jūzaburō had heard that Date Masamune (1567–1636), the original forefather of the domain, had insisted against all reason that what he built weren't castles but "strongholds, headquarters." This was sophistry, but the centrally located shogunate, inclined to leniency with the far-flung regions of Kyushu in the south and Michinoku in the north, let it pass. As a result, Sendai Domain was chock full of strongholds, each of which was allotted to a vassal as his headquarters. Yoshioka, having one such residence—Yoshioka Castle—had been granted to a vassal named Tadaki.

This grant had ultimately put Yoshioka at a disadvantage, Jūzaburō couldn't help thinking. Post towns had heavy burdens. Besides the regular land tax that all farmers had to pay, horses and labor had to be furnished for domanial use on the highway; men and horses could be forcibly confiscated. This burden was unjustly heavy, putting post towns at risk of ruin. The Date clan had taken the matter under advisement and come up with a remedy: a special subsidy for post towns to prevent their impoverishment.

There was one thing wrong with this remedy, and every time Jūzaburō thought of it, he felt a rush of anger: not a penny came to Yoshioka.

"Why does only our post town have to suffer like this? It's downright discrimination." The townspeople had been complaining for years, to no avail. The domain officials' reply was always the same: "Yoshioka land belongs to Tadaki, and you are subject to him. You are not subject to the daimyo, so you are not entitled to a subsidy from him." They wouldn't budge from this position. That was why Yoshioka inhabitants suffered such a crushing burden. During times of famine people drifted away, and the number of households dwindled. Fewer households meant a still heavier burden on those who remained—and so the population dwindled more.

The post town was caught in a vicious trap. Realizing this, Jūzaburō couldn't take the least pleasure in the sight of the peach blossom at the height of its beauty. Rather, the lovelier the spring sunshine, the emptier he felt.

Something had to be done. Jūzaburō walked along the irrigation ditch, racking his brains, but came up with nothing. Then a man's name occurred to him: Sugawaraya Tokuheiji. This person, a tea farmer, was reputed to be the wisest man in Yoshioka. Maybe he could think of a plan.

Yoshioka had long produced a great deal of tea. In fact, most of the tea drunk in Sendai Domain came from here. But outside the domain, people looked down on it, refusing to believe the northerly region was suited for tea cultivation. No fine tea could possibly come from the Kurokawa district of Michinoku, outsiders would tell Tokuheiji. He took this opinion in stride, convinced that he could produce tea as fine as that from Uji in Kyoto. He carefully nurtured his tea shrubs, and sure enough, in time he produced a tea every bit as good as Jōkisen, the choicest Uji tea. Yoshioka residents were amazed. Now at village assemblies and the like, Tokuheiji's opinions commanded respect.

Tokuheiji's shop was across the road diagonally from Kokudaya. Just the other day, right around the Doll Festival at the beginning of March, he had invited Jūzaburō over to taste his tea. Tokuheiji was thirty-five years old, exactly twelve years younger than Jūzaburō; they both were born in the Year of the Rat. Of their two establishments, Jūzaburō's was by far the more prosperous, but Tokuheiji was a man of such solid maturity and so knowledgeable that when they were together, it seemed as if their ages were reversed. Jūzaburō felt as if he were sitting at the feet of a teacher.

That evening Jūzaburō waited until dark and then made up his mind to go call on Tokuheiji. Since he had already been invited for a tasting, there was no reason to hesitate. He crossed the road and stood at the Sugawaraya gate.

The *Kokuonki*, the official record of the story, indicates that this visit occurred on the evening of March 5, 1766.

Tokuheiji's handmade specialty tea was delicious. Jūzaburō drank it in one gulp from a small teacup, and it left a delightful aftertaste. As soon as he finished it, Tokuheiji poured him a cup of another variety.

"Just a little is fine."

"Oh, but there's nothing I like more than having people drink my tea."

"In that case, I'll have more with pleasure."

"I raised five varieties this year, each one a slightly different flavor."

Jūzaburō drained his cup again. "Oh yes, this definitely is different. What fine tea! Yoshioka has something to be proud of."

Tokuheiji beamed. "Don't tell anyone, but I have a secret. I'll let you in on it. I'm going to present samples of my teas to Kujō Naozane, the chief advisor to the emperor."

Jūzaburō gasped. Tokuheiji was truly no ordinary man. Knowing that the only reason people looked down on Michinoku tea was because the site of cultivation was so far from the capital, he had decided to boost its prestige by sending some to the most powerful member of the Imperial Court. A brilliant solution. He had probably come up with it in an instant. Rather than standing in awe of the chief advisor's power, he intended to use that power to enhance the reputation of his tea. The boldness of the idea was thrilling and a bit terrifying.

"You're probably shocked," said Tokuheiji. "But I figure if you only wish for results, you'll spend your life wishing. Life is short. As things are, Yoshioka is headed for oblivion. We have to come up with a product to sell, or people here won't be able to make a living. I'll send my stuff to Kyoto to demonstrate the high quality of tea we have here. Doing that has to be good not only for my business but for our town."

He was right. Wishing couldn't change the future. Jūzaburō felt a surge of excitement. Here was his chance: face-to-face with this forward-looking man, he would reveal what lay on his mind. Words came pouring out.

"Actually, I came here tonight wondering if something can't be done."

"Oh?"

"These past few years, everywhere you go people are in distress, but here in Yoshioka it's even worse. More houses are abandoned every year. There are no buyers. People wouldn't take a house in Yoshioka if you paid them. We're in a terrible fix. How do you suppose this came to be?"

"Well," said Tokuheiji, "I share your concern, but since you've brought the matter up, let me first hear your thoughts."

Tokuheiji's answer was cautious and probing. He seemed afraid to commit himself, as if he might say something critical of the daimyo that would get him in trouble if he, Jūzaburō, reported it to the authorities. In that case there was nothing for it but to plunge ahead and tell all.

"Compared with the number of farmers and horses," said Jūzaburō, "there's never been much land in Yoshioka. The town has two hundred households, but few farmers have even two acres of land. Lots of people have a house but no land at all. People try to get along by engaging in business, but these days business is worse than ever. The markets held every five days are almost deserted. If you ask me, Yoshioka's going downhill faster than anywhere else."

"True," Tokuheiji agreed. "But there's more to it than that. Not only do we have less land, unlike other post towns we aren't entitled to a subsidy—yet we need it more. The daimyo is strapped for cash these days and sells lumber to raise money, chopping down all the trees in the interior. That lumber has to be transported, so the burden on us is many times greater than it used to be. People know that if they live here, their horses will be confiscated for the daimyo's use and their homes will lose value. That's the real reason why the town is becoming a ghost town."

Jūzaburō swallowed hard and looked around. What if someone were listening behind the door? The wrath of the authorities would fall on their heads. Tokuheiji had stated clearly the reason why the post town was suffering: the daimyo was to blame.

"What should we do?"

"I have a plan," said Tokuheiji, "though it's hardly my place to come up with one. My plan could save Yoshioka. But something else has to come first, and that's money. I don't have enough for what I have in mind."

"How much money do you figure it would take to save the town?"

Tokuheiji sighed. "One thousand four or five hundred ryō."

How could that fantastic sum of money save Yoshioka? Jūzaburō was bewildered. But if Tokuheiji said it was so, he must have a workable plan. Jūzaburō couldn't wait to hear what it was. "That much would be enough?"

"Yes. There is a way, but the money is essential. I can't commit highway robbery to save the town, of course, but sometimes I'm tempted. That's how desperately I need money."

"When you say save the town, do you mean everyone? If you know a way to ensure the town's prosperity indefinitely, we've got to do it, whatever the cost. Tell me what you're thinking. For years I've wondered if something couldn't be done. Won't you let me in on your plan?" What made Jūzaburō so insistent he couldn't have said, but he practically begged his friend to take him into his confidence. As he leaned forward to catch Tokuheiji's next words, he seemed to see the tea farmer in a halo of light.

"There's really not much to it." Tokuheiji said. "It's simple. We turn over the money to the daimyo and request that he pay us annual interest on the loan."

Jūzaburō stared in astonishment, instantly converted. The plan was brilliant: they would turn the tables by becoming creditors rather than debtors. Residents couldn't go on allowing themselves to be bled dry; instead they would band together to lend money to the 620,000-koku domain of Sendai. But would the daimyo accept such a proposal? A shadow of anxiety crossed his face.

Sensing his doubt, Tokuheiji assured him, "Remember, the daimyo himself is hard up. We'd aim for a time when he was especially hungry for cash. Just after he's ordered to donate money to the shogunate, say, or just before he has to set off on his biannual procession to Edo, that long, expensive journey with a huge entourage. If we make our proposal then, I'm sure he'll listen."

Probably so, Jūzaburō thought, nodding.

"Besides," Tokuheiji went on, "in the last few years the daimyo has started offering assistance to other post towns. You never know, he might even help us out by padding the interest. The going rate is ten percent a year. If we lent him one thousand ryō, we should receive nearly one hundred ryō in interest. If that money were distributed to every residence that has to furnish labor and horses for official use, Yoshioka could be in good shape indefinitely. If we don't act now, more families are sure to be driven out. Those of us who remain will be taxed to death. The thought of it gives me the chills. To keep that from happening, we need to scrape up one thousand ryō, all of us together.

"Mind you, I didn't come up with this idea on the spur of the moment. I've had it in the back of my mind for some time now, but it's so bold and requires so much capital that I knew I couldn't do it on my own. I let time slide without acting, just stewing in frustration. But as they say, where there's a will, there's a way. Nothing is impossible if you truly want it to happen. Negative thinking is a barrier to getting anything done. Talking with you has inspired me. I'll devote the rest of my life to this plan to save Yoshioka—and if I can't make it happen in this lifetime, I'll be reborn and make it happen in the next!"

Tokuheiji spoke with heat. Jūzaburō had known the younger man since he was a toddler, and never before had he heard him speak with such passion or seen such fierceness in his eyes. Listening, he was transfixed; his hair stood on end.

"That's it, Sugawaraya-san!" he cried. "You amaze me—I never knew you thought that way! Since you've shared your dreams with me, let me be honest, too. It's grated on me for a long time that our town's not entitled to a subsidy. The system is cruel. I've often wondered if there wasn't some way to amass a large sum of money, present it to the daimyo, and throw ourselves on his mercy. But I could never think of any way to do it. I've spent years doing nothing, just turning it over in my mind."

Now it was Tokuheiji's turn to be astonished. True, Jūzaburō's idea of making the daimyo a large payment as a way to dispose him to be merciful wasn't the same as making him a loan to receive a fixed amount of yearly interest; still, knowing that someone else in Yoshioka had been thinking along the same lines came as a revelation.

Jūzaburō went on, his eyes gleaming. The *Kokuonki* records his words as follows:

"Since you and I share the same desire, let's encourage one another. Let's strengthen our wills and work together without ever giving up this great dream of ours. Let's swear by all that is sacred that we'll make it come true. If we choose the right time, the heavens will bless us and we'll attain our goal in the end. Sometimes a single seed goes into the ground and doesn't decay, but leads to a thousand branches in blossom. We have to believe we can do it."

"You're right," said Tokuheiji. "The first step is strengthening our wills."

The two men had realized a great truth. The human heart is a seed—a seed that can open up a future without end. Just as a single seed has the power to transform an entire mountain, blanketing it in cherry blossoms, a strong will can accomplish miracles.

And yet Jūzaburō couldn't help feeling apprehensive. If they did lend money to the daimyo, would they really get anything back?

Tokuheiji didn't hesitate. "Naturally we wouldn't lend it directly to him. The money would go to Daimonjiya for investment, and our interest would be paid from there."

Daimonjiya served as the domain bank, lending money and managing and investing domain funds for the ruling Date clan. Jūzaburō was aware of this, and he also knew that Daimonjiya was more knowledgeable about domain finances than any official. If Daimonjiya handled the investment, payment of ten percent annual interest was assured. Instead of handling the thousand ryō themselves, they would deposit it with Daimonjiya, where the sum would be sure to increase. This was Tokuheiji's ingenious plan.

They couldn't invest the money directly in Yoshioka, Tokuheiji explained, because the town's decline was too rapid. Even if they amassed a thousand ryō, there'd be nowhere to invest it. What Yoshioka merchant could take one thousand ryō in capital and pay out one hundred ryō in interest year after year? In Sendai it was different. The castle town had plenty of samurai residences and townhouses with people in them just itching to borrow money.

The term "capital demand" did not yet exist, but if it had, it would have applied to samurai and wealthy merchants, the privileged classes of the time. Samurai took forty percent of total rice production and used it for consumption. Their demand for funds was considerable. Capital demand was also high among Sendai's official purveyors, sake and oil dealers who handled the annual tribute rice used for taxation. In the Edo period, all those in control of distribution and brewing and in the business of lending money to samurai were wealthy and in need of capital.

The keeper of the warehouse would commonly procure capital at ten percent interest and lend it out to samurai at nearly double that rate. With a nearly ten percent profit margin, it might seem as if lenders were raking in money hand over fist, but lending money to samurai wasn't for everyone. This was widely understood, as samurai were notorious for failing to pay their debts. Getting a samurai to pay off a debt was extremely difficult because samurai land and houses were all bestowed by the daimyo and so could never be sold or mortgaged. No merchant creditor had ever succeeded in taking the land of a feudal retainer and acquiring the status of feudal retainer himself. To lend money to a samurai, you had to be able to seize his annual grant of rice. This meant developing connections with *kurayakunin*, direct representatives of the daimyo in charge of warehouse quarters, and getting them to accommodate you by allowing you to take what you were owed before they delivered the rice. Only those able to pull off this trick could lend money to samurai.

Tokuheiji suggested that they have the keeper of the warehouse handle their loan and set up a system for money to flow from Sendai to Yoshioka. "That way we farmers can get our tribute rice back from the samurai who took it from us."

Jūzaburō couldn't help nodding in admiration. But Tokuheiji was still young. Jūzaburō felt suddenly ill at ease. As a precaution, he said, "You know, Sugawaraya-san, you have a slight tendency to be talkative. Keep this discussion under your hat for now. Whatever you do, don't let on to other people about it and make yourself a laughingstock."

"Oh dear," said Tokuheiji. "You know me too well!"

The two men shared a laugh and parted amicably.

Change begins with a glimmer inside someone's head. Usually such glimmers disappear like the light snow that falls in spring, but now and then one will catch on and grow to surprising size, becoming so big that it changes everything. That is how history unfolds, and that evening's conversation between the two men marked just such a beginning.

The idea was perhaps preposterous. "If we keep on as we are, the annual taxes will bleed us dry. Samurai will suck the marrow from our bones and toss them aside. Let's change things around so that we're the ones taking money from them." This was the momentous decision reached by Kokudaya Jūzaburō and Sugawaraya Tokuheiji on that night of March 5, 1766.

Quietly they would gather like-minded people, raise one thousand ryō and lend it to the lord of Sendai, then collect one hundred ryō in interest each year and distribute it to the townspeople. This would be the salvation of Yoshioka.

The residents of Yoshioka would become moneylenders to the daimyo and squeeze money from him. That was the long and the short of it. Such a plan could be considered dangerous. If it were carelessly leaked, village officials might bring the two of them to justice. Jūzaburō proceeded cautiously, knowing he was on thin ice.

Conspirators were as despised as snakes. If three or more people gathered in secret and talked about the government, they were considered a faction guilty of treason. The three centuries of peace under the Tokugawa shogunate were predicated on preventing people—everyone from daimyo to commoners—from forming horizontal connections and hatching schemes. The word *tō*, meaning party or faction, was strongly suggestive of wrongdoing. Since for three centuries Japanese people were conditioned not to form factions, in the Meiji period the concept of government by political parties was predictably difficult to grasp. That difficulty was to plague Japan's party politics for a very long time.

In any case, only two kinds of groups formed by horizontal connections existed in the Edo period: the villages people were born into and religious groups affiliated with a shrine or temple. Anything that could be construed as "gathering for the purpose of scheming against the government," an act of rebellion or treason, was fraught with danger.

Jūzaburō, though aware of the danger, was chafing with impatience.

"I know you're anxious to get started," said his friend, "but we have to pick the right time."

Already nearly six months had passed since their first meeting. They had met in secret several more times since then, but the plan was going nowhere.

"Well then, tell me this. Just when do you think will be the right time?"

"When the daimyo stands in greatest need of money."

"Then why not now? He's always broke."

"There's where you're wrong. Daimyo may seem to be broke, but they never really are. Think about it. Did you ever hear of a daimyo going bankrupt because of his debts? What they fear most is not having enough money to respond when the shogunate calls on them to do something."

"Yes, if a daimyo couldn't fulfill his duty to the shogunate, that would be the end of him. The whole country would know of his humiliation."

"Right. And that's how we seize the advantage—if I dare say such a thing. Just wait, Jūzaburō. Sooner or later an order from the shogunate will have our daimyo desperate for cash. Then we make our move."

Jūzaburō was forced to admit the wisdom of this approach.

Ordinarily, no matter what they said to domain authorities, they would be turned down. But if they waited until the domain was saddled with some fiscally taxing burden and perilously low on funds, the domain would have no choice but to agree.

"A drowning man will clutch at a straw," said Tokuheiji. "So will a daimyo." He laughed.

Their opportunity came surprisingly soon—too soon, in fact. In August 1766, Yoshioka was swept by a rumor: the lord of Sendai had been ordered to aid riparian work in Kantō. The burden on the domain would be passed on to the farmers, who naturally grumbled. To Jūzaburō, however, this was their long-awaited chance. Unable to suppress his excitement, he ran over to Tokuheiji's place. He couldn't wait to share the good news.

"Sugawaraya-san! It's time! The daimyo has been ordered to assist in shoring up rivers."

But Tokuheiji's expression was morose. "This is terrible. I never expected our chance to come so soon. There's no way we can raise that kind of money in time."

"But it's the perfect chance!"

"For the domain to even consider our proposal, we've got to make a significant offer. Without at least a thousand ryō in hand, there's no point in even trying. Have we got that much?"

"We could appeal to others…"

"Yes, we need to bring more people in, that's true. But it's got to be done cautiously or we could land in serious trouble."

Indeed they could. The domain would be imposing another heavy burden on inhabitants who were already gasping for breath. Fearing an eruption of popular discontent, officials were on the alert for any sign of conspiracy or rebellion. If the two men weren't careful, someone might turn them in to the authorities, and they could land in prison. All their plans would come to nothing.

"All I can think of to do now is pray," said Tokuheiji.

Since a man of his wisdom said this, Jūzaburō too had no recourse but to appeal for divine help. From that day on, he resolved to forgo hot baths. There was a public bath in Yoshioka where in warm weather he enjoyed going to wash off the sweat of the day, but he forfeited this pleasure and instead poured cold water over himself in a daily ritual of purification. To his satisfaction, Tokuheiji did the same.

The *Kokuonki* says, "They ceased going to the public bath, as was their custom, and poured cold water over themselves morning and evening. In between, they fasted and prayed." In this way they saved the cost of going to the public bath and also saved money by fasting. People began to wonder what they were up to. Anyone undergoing such ritual purification was assumed to have some deep reason. But since their plan involved the lord of Sendai, they couldn't tell anyone about it. All they could do was pray with all their might. This was to have an unexpected effect, but at the time they had no way of knowing that. They simply kept on dousing themselves with cold water and praying.

They soon ran into difficulty. People began to look askance at them. "Something's wrong with Kokudaya Jūzaburō and Sugawaraya Tokuheiji. All that abstinence—they'll be lucky if they don't make themselves sick."

Tokuheiji decided they couldn't afford to risk letting their plan be known. The time had come to talk things over with Chisaka Chūnai.

The Chisaka family of Yoshioka held the hereditary post of district headman for all Kurokawa County. The district headman was the highest-ranking local official chosen from among the farmers. The current holder of that office, a thirty-year-old named Chūnai, was the person in town closest to the daimyo—in a sense, his agent. Tokuheiji now proposed letting him in on their plan. Jūzaburō thought he was mad to consider it, but Tokuheiji reminded him that they had little chance of success otherwise. He had a point. If Chisaka Chūnai didn't approve their plan, that would be that. The district headman was the linchpin of local administration—the one and only connection to the daimyo. If they couldn't go through him, they would have to petition the lord themselves. But to go over the head of the district headman and appeal directly to the lord or other high officials was a serious offense, possibly punishable by death. Unless they followed the proper procedure, their appeal would fail. Clearly, they had to start out by approaching Chūnai and winning him over. His cooperation was crucial.

A surprising thing about samurai government in the Edo period was that civil administration was left almost entirely in the hands of the people. Daimyo families were essentially military in orientation. Samurai could be sent directly to the villages to rule them as headmen, but that was seldom done, except in Satsuma and a few other domains. The farmers would almost certainly have rebelled. Under the samurai government, as long as farmers paid their land tax, they were left alone. There was no need to interfere in village affairs, and villagers were content to have no interference. Mutual understanding between the samurai and the farmers produced the headman system and the *murauke* system, a self-governing system of rural taxation. Influential farmers were chosen to collect village-wide taxes and govern. Above the village headman was the district headman, one for every ten villages or so—the most powerful local official.

Above the latter was the county magistrate, a position held by a domain samurai, together with a local magistrate, but all actual work was done by people at a lower level. If an order went out to do a census, for example, it was their job to make family registers and count heads. The magistrates would do nothing but sit in their seats of honor and listen to reports.

District headman Chisaka Chūnai handled all civil affairs in Kurokawa County. Anything that Jūzaburō and his supporters wanted to do therefore had to have his support.

The Chisaka family was known for being generous to a fault—a trait that once very nearly bankrupted them. Chūnai's father, as a young man, had been undisciplined. He guzzled sake, which drove his mother wild. One day she told him: "Some people are so poor they can't afford to drink sake, and that's all you do!" Strange to tell, from that day on he gave up drinking and started buying up medicine and distributing it to the poor. He paid funeral fees for those unable to afford them and gave money to couples who couldn't afford to get married. During a drought he had an irrigation ditch dug for the village with his own funds, plunging the Chisaka family into poverty and nearly causing them to be stripped of their hereditary position. The townspeople never forgot his kindness, and little by little they paid off the family's debts. And now the man's son and grandson were their representatives.

Chūnai was known for his integrity. In old age his father had grown senile and often wandered off, but rather than leave him in other people's hands, he and his wife looked after him themselves. "Chisaka Chūnai has important official duties and can't tend to his father, who's always disappearing. That's why he has servants watch over him. But if his father isn't back by dark, he'll stand in the doorway, anxiously waiting. If his father's footwear is dirty, he'll clean it himself." All this was common knowledge. Jūzaburō and Tokuheiji wouldn't have consulted the town headman, but Chisaka Chūnai they thought might listen.

One night under cover of dark the two men called at the Chisaka residence and told Chūnai about their plan. Chūnai sat and listened, his mouth in a straight line. The light in a floor lantern wavered as Tokuheiji talked on at length. When he was finished, an appallingly long silence enveloped the three men. Jūzaburō and Tokuheiji held their breath, waiting for some response. But Chūnai, despite having had this momentous plan confided to him, said not a word. Their hearts sank.

But then Chūnai's thick lips moved. Tears were in his eyes as he spoke. "These days, people often come here by night with secret requests. Until now, they've all come on their own behalf. When they say they want to give his lordship a large sum of money, usually it's because they want to be made samurai in return. They want to raise their station in life by having him grant them a fief or a stipend. Only men like that have ever come here. Since you two also proposed giving his lordship a large sum of money, I assumed you had a similar scheme in mind, but having heard you out, I realize that what you're proposing is different. You want to do something for people who can't make a living in Yoshioka. You've had that thought in mind for some time and this evening, not knowing where else to turn, you finally came to me. I understand and applaud your goal. I can't think of a nobler deed. I have just one request. From this night on, allow me to join you and work alongside you."

And so the three men pledged to join forces to save Yoshioka.

Jūzaburō once asked Tokuheiji, "You say we're going to lend a thousand ryō to the domain and use the interest to revitalize Yoshioka. Whose approval exactly do we need? Surely not the daimyo himself?"

"No, not him. There are six magistrates in the Date clan. All we need is their okay."

"How can we possibly get all six to grant us permission?"

"Ah. There are six, but we really only need the permission of one. Samurai would far rather be involved in military defense or even the upkeep of temples and shrines. Only one magistrate is involved with county administration work, or finance, which is the least desirable work in the shogunate."

"I see. Then he's the one who'll decide whether or not our request is taken up?"

"No."

Jūzaburō was silent, waiting.

"He's so eminent, he's probably never made a purchase in his life. There's someone else called the comptroller. The decision will be his."

"The comptroller, is he an eminent man too?"

"Very. Above our district headman is the magistrate; above him is the county magistrate, and above him are the comptroller and the rest. The present comptroller is a man named Kayaba Moku. Lowly people like you and me can't possibly approach him."

"Who can?"

"Hm. I doubt if even Chisaka-sama could get an audience with him. Only the magistrate would be allowed to see him."

Jūzaburō felt faint. If they did somehow manage to raise the money, they would have to negotiate with the highest authorities in the domain to create a system whereby Yoshioka alone could receive a special annuity. It seemed beyond the realm of the possible. Even though their plan was entirely unselfish, conceived for the good of the town as a whole, domain officials disliked doing anything unprecedented. Getting them to go along with this plan would be as hard as digging up the nearby hills and carting them away.

Jūzaburō hadn't taken even his son, Otoemon, into his confidence. The two weren't close. In fact, Otoemon wasn't Jūzaburō's own child. Instead, he'd been adopted into the Kokudaya family as heir, like Jūzaburō before him. Otoemon was diligent and had a good head on his shoulders, but he and Jūzaburō never talked about anything but work. They had never had a real conversation. It wasn't that they didn't get along or held different values; they simply never exchanged any unnecessary words, and each worked steadily at the family business. Every day, this father and son who were no blood relation knelt side by side before the memorial tablets of Kokudaya family ancestors, lit incense and prayed for the safety and prosperity of their adoptive family.

The name Kokudaya was the family *yagō*, not a true surname indicating blood relations but a name taken from the business (the *ya* of *yagō* and of Kokudaya and Sugawaraya means "shop"). The Kokudaya family also had a surname, "Takahira." This wasn't an official surname granted by the domain but a hidden one they used privately among themselves. They couldn't put it on official forms, but in private correspondence they wrote their names like samurai: "Takahira Otoemon." All the merchant families of any standing in Yoshioka did this.

In any case, what Jūzaburō was now seeking to do was, from the perspective of the Kokudaya family, preposterous. Far from ensuring stability, it could wipe out the family fortune. If he succeeded, Yoshioka might prosper, but the family business might well go belly up. If Otoemon, his serious-minded son, knew any of this, what would he think? It pained Jūzaburō to imagine. They had to proceed carefully, step by step, or the plan would fail.

One day in May 1768, Jūzaburō suddenly called out to Otoemon: "I'm going to go see Jūbei. Come with me."

"What are you going for, Father?"

"You'll see. Come along."

Otoemon had no choice but to accompany him to the home of Kokudaya Jūbei, a relative of theirs. After they arrived, Jūzaburō began to talk. He told Jūbei and Otoemon that he and Tokuheiji were planning to lend one thousand ryō to the lord and collect interest; that the district headman was aboard the plan; that they still had no idea how to raise the money; and that he was prepared to sacrifice Kokudaya, if need be, to make it work. He talked, and Jūbei listened in silence. Otoemon too said nothing. Perhaps they were won over by the force of justice in his words. As Jūzaburō talked on with urgency, his face showed not a trace of hesitation. There was a kind of magical strength in him. The other two listened without comment to this plan that could well prove their undoing and enmesh them in woe.

When Jūzaburō was finished, once again something unbelievable happened.

"Jūzaburō, bravo," said Jūbei. "I don't think your plan has a chance of success—but you might as well try. I believe that good deeds are under divine protection. That must be why you gave up taking hot baths and instead douse yourself with cold water. Keep on, don't give up, and never waver. Wait for the right time. In the meantime, let me join you."

Overjoyed, Jūzaburō gripped Jūbei's hand tightly in his. Then he turned to Otoemon. "I'm nearly fifty now," he said. "I doubt if I can see this plan through in my lifetime. If I should die before it comes about, I want you to take over for me and see that everyone works together to make it happen. Even when my body decays and disintegrates, my spirit will hover over you and give you strength. This plan will succeed."

"Father," said Otoemon, "this is the first time I've ever seen into your heart. Now I understand what's been weighing on you all this time. This is a noble ambition. I'll remember your words not just after you're gone, but now, while you're alive. I'll never let you down."

And so Otoemon too pledged his commitment to the cause and proceeded to devote himself to it even more than Jūzaburō. The father and son that had always been rather distant now shared a bond as strong as that between real fathers and sons, or stronger. The rest of the family and the neighbors, not knowing what had brought the two of them together, could only look on and wonder.

Jūzaburō's and Tokuheiji's preparations were nearly complete.

The population of Japan at this time was thirty million, with some six million households. There were fifty thousand villages across Japan, with a headman in each one. If there was more than one landowner in a village, or if the village was exceptionally large, there might be several. The total number of headmen and their families was around five hundred thousand. Approximately one in every fifty farmers was a town headman.

In contrast, the population of samurai families was around 1.5 million, three times greater. But samurai were of no use during times of peace, so across Japan, the five hundred thousand headmen and their families looked after the people. In that sense, they were the mainstay of Japan. Moreover, they represented a fount of knowledge.

In the mid-eighteenth century, as Japan was emerging from its long slumber, few people could be considered learned, even though that meant little more than the ability to read Chinese and convey one's thoughts in writing. The most literate segment of the population consisted of the samurai, the headmen, and members of the clergy—Shinto priests and Buddhist monks. Village headmen in particular were organizers of culture in the villages. To farmers, they were government administrators, teachers, and literati as well as sources of information on the wider world.

No country can manage without rational people. If Japan's five hundred thousand village headmen not been men of reason, the country would almost certainly have met a dismal fate.

In any case, the town headman was crucial to their plans. Without the aid of a man named Endō Ikuemon, Jūzaburō and the others would never make any headway.

"It's time to let Ikuemon know what's going on," Jūzaburō said. "We went to Chūnai over his head. How should we bring up the subject?"

"There's nothing to worry about," Tokuheiji assured him. "Ikuemon isn't one to make waves. As long as Chūnai is for it, he'll cooperate. If there's a consensus, he'll say yes to anything. That's the sort of man he is. But we certainly don't want to do anything to put his nose out of joint. Rather than convincing him with logic, it'd be better to go drinking together and appeal to his emotions."

"You're right," said Jūzaburō, impressed as usual with Tokuheiji's sense. "He may not be a thinker, but he has a good heart."

"Where could we get treated to drinks?"

"I know a place." Jūzaburō was always welcome to drink at his brother's home.

Ikuemon loved to drink, and besides, he and Jūzaburō were kin. His surname was Endō, making him a member of a branch family of the Asanoya. The Endō family, with its connections to the Asanoya, was known in Yoshioka as a distinguished line founded by Endō Izumi no kami. The local temple, Kuhonji, had a gravestone marked in bold letters with his name. Legend had it that the

Asanoya family was descended from a daimyo. The reason Ikuemon had the job of headman in the first place was through his connection to this branch family. As a result, he was deeply indebted to the main Asanoya family and felt a bond with Jūzaburō—a connection too good to waste.

They decided they would invite him to the main branch of the Asanoya family, get him good and drunk, and then tell him what they had in mind.

Asanoya wealth was conspicuous in Yoshioka. The family owned a grand house on the broad avenue running through town, and brewery after brewery. They produced three different brands of sake; no other brewer in the vicinity came close to them. Their drinking parties were known for their extravagance.

With the family's permission, Jūzaburō invited Ikuemon to one such party. He came gladly, and just as they'd intended, he soon got pleasantly tipsy; but even when the evening was nearly over, they still hadn't been able to broach the crucial topic with him. There were too many people around, and nowhere to have a private chat.

At one point Jūzaburō lost patience and started to bear down on the town headman, eyes gleaming with determination, but Tokuheiji signaled him to stop.

Soon it was time to go home. Jūzaburō fretted, not wanting to let Ikuemon go home yet, not until they had talked to him. As he stood helplessly by, Tokuheiji went sauntering up to Ikuemon, who was clearly enjoying himself.

"Ikuemon," he said, "are you sure you had enough to drink here?"

"Well, now that you mention it... How about if we go to my place? Jūzaburō, thanks for inviting me tonight. Why don't you come too? What do you say, Tokuheiji?"

"If you insist!" Tokuheiji looked and sounded as pleased as could be. He glanced back at Jūzaburō and grinned as if to say, "See? That's how it's done."

In the home of town headman Ikuemon, they did some serious drinking.

Ikuemon was a bighearted man who liked to look after others. He had a young son and heir named Tōkichi, and whenever he was in his cups he would fret about his son's future. Tonight too, as the night wore on the talk turned to what the future might hold for young Tōkichi.

Ikuemon had every reason to be worried. In Yoshioka, rendering the annual land tax and supplying post horses were increasingly difficult. Tax-collecting was the duty of the town headman, and if Yoshioka defaulted, he and Tōkichi would both be thrown into prison. They would be put in a cage exposed to the elements, one thin cotton kimono apiece their only protection from the cold winter winds. Tōkichi would certainly freeze to death.

Though he tried not to think about it, Ikuemon sensed doom creeping steadily closer. That was why lately he had taken to drink.

"Is there no way out?" he muttered, drink in hand, his face flushed.

Tokuheiji didn't let slip the chance to tell him about their plan: by raising one thousand ryō and lending it to the daimyo, the town could escape the heavy burden of taxation.

For a moment, Ikuemon looked stunned. Then, "If you need to raise money for that," he said with tears in his eyes, "I would gladly sell all my furniture and belongings. I would carry a sack and go begging. My wife and I could become someone's servants. Tōkichi would be better off that way." He meant every word.

"I know how you feel," said Jūzaburō. "When I think of the future, when your Tōkichi will be a man ready to take his place as town headman, I too feel an urgent need to do something. As it is, our children don't stand a chance."

"That's right," said Ikuemon, "and yet..."

"And yet what?"

"Does a scheme this wild stand any chance of success?"

That was the question. How much chance did their plan have, realistically speaking? Jūzaburō had never come out and asked Tokuheiji this, but he too wanted to know.

"Certainly it won't be easy," said Tokuheiji. "I'd say we're like monkeys reaching for the moon." With his face as red as a monkey's from drinking, he said this in a humorous way that immediately released the tension, and they all burst out laughing.

Could monkeys grab the moon? There was no way to know without trying. The three men resolved to take the plunge. And so Jūzaburō and Tokuheiji succeeded in getting the town headman to join them. This was in May 1768.

Two months later, on one hot midsummer's day Jūzaburō received a letter. The sender's name was written on the envelope: "Miuraya Sōemon, Yanagi-machi, Sendai." This was serious business. Miuraya was a merchant who did business with the daimyo, which made him the biggest magnate in the castle town and hence in the domain, someone far above a country merchant like himself. With trembling hands, Jūzaburō opened the envelope. The letter was written in Miuraya's own hand.

> I have been ordered to mint money. A large staff will be needed for the task. His lordship has told me to find fourteen or fifteen men of good character. Would it be possible to have your son and heir, Otoemon, become overseer? I realize I have no right to make this request, but I can think of no one I would rather have do the job. I have full confidence in Otoemon's character. I therefore earnestly request his assistance.

This came as a complete surprise. Jūzaburō was unsure what to do. The domain was going to mint its own coins, and Miuraya was asking for his son to lend a hand.

One notable thing about the Edo period was that the country didn't mint its own currency, but left the task to ordinary merchants. Coins known as Kan'ei tsūhō, cast in copper or iron, had recently begun circulating, but the shogunate, Japan's central government, had nothing to do with the issuing of this basic currency. Minting coins was permitted even for "outside" daimyo—descendants of those who had opposed the victorious Tokugawa at the battle of Sekigahara in 1600. Of course, permission was required, but that was mere window dressing. Daimyo who minted coins did so because they were in financial difficulty and had desperate need of cash. They did it completely on their own. Moreover, the domain itself did not undertake the minting directly but commissioned wealthy merchants to do the job. Thus the responsibility for something of great importance to the nation was passed from the shogunate to the domains, and from the domains to the merchants. In Sendai, this responsibility rested with Miuraya.

The shogunate's custom of handing over the minting of coins to the domains led to trouble as Satsuma and other domains issued counterfeit currency to fatten their coffers. Kan'ei tsūhō were worth only one mon apiece (about fifty yen, or half a US dollar), but coins called Tempōsen were worth one hundred times as much. Various domains profited enormously by privately minting Tempōsen in the closing years of the Tokugawa regime. In allowing domains to mint coins, the shogunate let down its guard and so shortened its life.

In any case, this letter was a serious matter. Jūzaburō rushed to tell Tokuheiji the news. Tokuheiji's response was unexpected: he danced for joy.

"Jūzaburō, this is wonderful! It's a one in a million chance. Now we monkeys may actually get our hands on the moon!"

Jūzaburō was stunned into silence.

"Finally the lord is pressed for money," explained Tokuheiji, "and has started to mint coins. Of course we must be part of this. Miuraya Sōemon is purveyor to the domain, and your son has come into his favor. A mint overseer is an upstanding government official. If he takes this job, Otoemon will definitely earn the lord's trust."

"So you're saying that for Otoemon to work for the domain would be to our advantage?"

"Absolutely. This changes everything. And that's not all. There's money in it."

"Surely not."

"Don't you see? Miuraya may be the wealthiest man in all Sendai, but you don't think he mints coins at his own expense, do you?"

"No, I suppose not."

"Starting up a mint is hugely expensive. You have to construct buildings for the purpose, gather workers, purchase copper, build furnaces, lay in plenty of firewood. It costs a small fortune. So in the beginning, Miuraya will go into the red—but that will soon change. He'll be making money hand over fist, so of course he's going to profit. That's what we'll have our eye on."

"How so?"

"Since Miuraya will need money at first, we'll lend it to him, and afterwards have him pay us back with a little extra thrown in."

"We can do that?"

"Of course! There's no better way to make money than to be a moneylender. And if we help him out, Miuraya will owe us a debt of gratitude, too. Once his mint gets rolling, he'll be even wealthier than he is now. Then we apply to him for a nice fat loan and use the money to revive Yoshioka."

"I get it."

"And if you let him have Otoemon, then we'll always know exactly what's going on. Miuraya may have chosen Otoemon because he admires his character, but I'll bet he also plans to borrow money from you, knowing you have quite a bit stashed away. That wouldn't surprise me in the least. I'd say by the end of this year he'll come to you and ask for a loan. You'd better be prepared."

What a shrewd mind the man had! Jūzaburō marveled at this far-sightedness. It struck him as almost uncanny.

So Jūzaburō agreed to Miuraya's request and sent his son to head the mint. And then everything unfolded just as Tokuheiji had said it would. First Miuraya came to Jūzaburō for a loan. This happened at the end of the year, just as Tokuheiji had foreseen. He asked for five hundred and fifty ryō to pay workers' wages and purchase lumber, adding that a high-interest loan "wouldn't be a problem."

Tokuheiji acted swiftly. He sent off a messenger to the home of district headman Chisaka Chūnai and gathered the contributors—Chūnai, Ikuemon, Jūbei, Junai, and the rest—to explain the next step. "For us to raise a thousand ryō on our own would be difficult if not impossible," he told them. "We need to lend Miuraya five hundred fifty ryō now so that later on we can borrow a larger sum from him."

"Is this really going to work?" Some of the men were unconvinced that the idea was sound.

"It'll take time for the mint to get up and running," Tokuheiji admitted. "But mark my words, this is a godsend. Ignore a godsend at your peril, they say. We need to commit ourselves."

"This could be the start of all we have dreamed," Jūzaburō chimed in. Together the two men "spoke with one tongue," in the *Kokuonki*'s vivid phrase and brought everyone to an agreement.

If they were going to lend money to Miuraya, they had to raise it quickly. Their trust in the business of minting might be weak, but they had strong faith in Miuraya. Money lent to him was bound to come back, they reassured one another. Morning and night, they worked to sort out their household goods, mortgaging their clothes and even their homes.

Tokuheiji pawned everything he owned, including his book of secrets in the art of making tea. "Surely you don't have to go that far," objected Jūzaburō, but Tokuheiji wouldn't listen. Even more amazingly, he pawned something he valued almost as much as life itself.

Sugawaraya tea had a marvelous fragrance, and it was known now even in Kyoto, where the chief advisor to the emperor had written out a poem in its honor, incorporating the names of all five varieties:

Spring breeze
Fragrance
From a thousand years,
As blossom waves cover
Sue no Matsuyama.

The five varieties were "Spring Breeze," "Fragrance," "Thousand Years," "Blossom Waves," and "Sue no Matsuyama," the name of a local mountain. Tokuheiji took even this poem, written in the chief advisor's own hand, and deposited it in the pawnshop.

When Jūzaburō heard this, he was incredulous. "Are you sure you want to pawn something that means so much to you?"

"Absolutely," Tokuheiji replied. "At a time like this, you have to give up something so valuable that people are set back on their heels. That's how you make them take what you're doing seriously."

And so they managed to raise the sum of four hundred and fifty ryō. This was the money that would prime the pump, leading to the revival of Yoshioka.

Soon it was New Year's, 1769. The sixteenth day of the New Year was *yabuiri*, the servants' holiday, when workers and apprentices in towns across the archipelago were allowed to return home. There was a saying: "At *yabuiri*, lids come off the cauldrons of Hell." The idea was that on that day the devils in Hell took a rest from their task of tormenting sinners, so those in this world could have the day off, too. In Yoshioka all the pots and kettles in town went lidless. Servant women responsible for cooking meals were sent home, and no one so much as boiled water. Bathhouses and barbers closed up shop.

Otoemon came home to the unusually quiet town from the mint in Ishinomaki, bringing welcome news. "The mint is in full swing," he reported. "Miuraya Sōemon is definitely making money."

Jūzaburō hurried to tell Tokuheiji. "Good news!" he cried. "Otoemon just came home. He says Miuraya is making money every time he turns around."

"He is? That rat!"

Jūzaburō waited.

"He's going to mint coins, he says, so he needs workers and cash, and he even takes your son Otoemon into the bargain and works him to the bone. Plus, he wangles a loan for his business from us, promising to pay us back out of his guaranteed profits."

"He also said he didn't care how high the interest was on the loan."

"Yes, but now he's changed his tune. Now it's 'laws constrain me,' 'I can't pay you,' 'I need more time.' All nonsense. If he's really raking it in, then he can afford to pay us back. Let's go to Ishinomaki and settle this."

"You mean, get back the money we lent him six months ago?"

"No. That goes without saying. We'll get back the four hundred and fifty ryō plus interest, and on top of that we'll have him lend us the remainder. That's how we'll get our thousand ryō from Miuraya."

"That sounds daft! Can we do such a thing?"

"Why do you ask? We made a deal with him, didn't we?"

Indeed they had. "If I make a profit from minting," Miuraya had said, "I promise to supply the funds needed for the revival of Yoshioka."

Once again Jūzaburō marveled at the workings of Tokuheiji's mind—the precision and boldness of his thinking. So far, everything he said had turned out to be true. Chances were good that he was also right about this. There was nothing to do but follow his lead.

"You think the odds are in our favor?" Jūzaburō asked timidly on the way to Ishinomaki.

"You're kin to Miuraya, aren't you?"

Miuraya might be a big man in the castle town of Sendai, but he had a father born in Yoshioka and relatives all around town, Jūzaburō among them. That blood connection was a main reason why Miuraya had sought the help of Jūzaburō's son.

"His lordship won't make any money through the minting of coins. It's the one who undertakes the job who profits. That's how it works. Miuraya is in a position now to pay us the thousand ryō, but prosperous merchants like him are crafty. They purposely lie low. They get by without paying as long as they can; they won't pay until you come after them. It's that simple."

"Yes, but…"

"Now, think. What happens if Miuraya causes trouble with us over work he was assigned by the daimyo? He fixed his seal to a bond. Scrapping that would affect his good name. Proprietors of large stores like his are especially concerned about keeping up appearances. Besides, he's from Yoshioka. If he abandoned our town to its fate, he'd find it awkward to come visit his ancestors' graves."

This made sense. If Miuraya reneged on his promise, it would be a black mark against his name. Tokuheiji had factored Miuraya's concern with appearances into the negotiations.

"The only way to handle something like this is to do it boldly, in the limelight. So, Jūzaburō, we need to set the stage. Help me."

Tokuheiji stuck a hand in the bosom of his kimono and pulled out a strange-looking piece of paper printed with a design of crows, held to be the sacred messengers of Kumano Shrine. By ancient tradition, those making a solemn vow would write it out on a sheet of this "crow-paper." Every time such a vow was broken, somewhere it was said, a crow died, kindling the wrath of Kumano Gongen (the shrine's object of worship). The oath-breaker would then vomit blood, die, and suffer the torments of hellfire. Tokuheiji had managed to get hold of some crow-paper and was now thrusting it at Jūzaburō.

As soon as they arrived at the mint in Ishinomaki, they had a face-to-face meeting with Miuraya Sōemon. Also assembled were gold engravers from Edo, other financiers, and mint staff. In a large hall filled with dignitaries, Tokuheiji launched into a speech.

"Miuraya-san put his seal on the promissory note you see here. Yet he now claims he is unable to honor his word and pay us the amount indicated."

This declaration was met with dead silence. Was he going to publicly censure Miuraya for being in the wrong?

Tokuheiji broke the silence. "Although by rights we deserve to be paid, we choose to forfeit our right. The fact is, five or six of us have banded together to do something to save the town of Yoshioka. We plan to offer a large sum of money to his lordship and receive yearly interest on the loan, for distribution among the townsfolk. This is the system we hope to set up. The money we lent Miuraya-san was a crucial part of that plan. The town of Yoshioka is poor, and we can't raise a fortune on our own. That's why we hoped to borrow money from the mint with Miuraya-san's help. We meant to pay him back out of the interest we received from the daimyo. But that's all in the past. All we ask now is for the return of the original 450 ryō we lent him last winter. We won't insist on the agreed rate of interest, either. The going rate will do."

"Well now," said Miuraya, squirming, "there's no need to be that way."

"In that case," said Tokuheiji, "let me put it before you again. Please lend us the money. I'm not saying we need it immediately. But if the mint prospers, let us have the money as promised. If the mint fails to prosper, then it's too bad, but we understand and we won't pursue the matter."

Clearly, Tokuheiji and the others were in the right and Miuraya and his supporters were in the wrong. Everyone present saw the logic of what he was saying. When Miuraya needed to make the mint, the people of Yoshioka had helped out, scraping together the little money each one had. If business was now going well, it was only fair for Miuraya to keep his promise, return the money he owed, and save the post town.

Then Tokuheiji slowly pulled out a document—the oath sworn on Kumano crow-paper.

"We hereby swear," he said, "we won't use one cent of the money we borrow for our own profit. We're not acting out of self-interest. Unless something is done, Yoshioka will dry up and blow away. All we want to do is prevent the worst from happening. We swear it to the three main Kumano Shrines."

He spread out the paper and prostrated himself before it. The oath was signed "Sugawaraya Tokuheiji" and "Kokudaya Jūzaburō," and it also bore the fingerprints of each man, as they had sealed the document in blood.

The eyes of everyone in the room turned to Miuraya. He stammered, "W-well, if that's how it is, I agree. I'm sure no one present has any objection."

And so it was settled. Miuraya would return the 450 ryō with interest. What's more, to support the recovery of Yoshioka he would lend them another 562 ryō and 2 bu. It all worked out perfectly.

"Tokuheiji, you are amazing!" Jūzaburō exclaimed. "You got him to lend us over a thousand ryō!"

Tokuheiji dismissed this praise, his mouth in a tight line. "Our work isn't finished. What we need isn't a verbal promise but a sworn written statement."

But Miuraya seemed to realize he was cornered. In April when Jūzaburō called at his kinsman's home in Yanagimachi, Sendai, Miuraya was pleasantly accommodating.

"Very soon now," said Jūzaburō, "we will be petitioning his lordship. To do that, we have to have the money in hand. I'd like to ask you to provide a written statement that you will furnish the necessary funds as promised."

"Of course, with pleasure." He agreed with disarming ease.

"Thank you very much."

"To whom should I address it?"

"To Sugawaraya Tokuheiji, Kokudaya Jūbei, and myself."

"Fine."

"You should know that if there is something goes wrong and we don't receive the five hundred and sixty-two ryō from you, the three of us will be forced to sell our household possessions and put our families into bondage."

This revelation startled Miuraya, whose life had been devoted solely to the pursuit of profit. He became suddenly talkative. "Yoshioka is where my late father was from. You and I come from different branches on the same family tree. I've always wondered if there wasn't something I could do for you. I'm very impressed with the project you and the others have come up with, and happy to be part of it."

And on and on he talked. Nothing he said was from the heart, but even knowing this, good-natured Jūzaburō was content just to hear him say the words.

Now they had half the capital they needed to support their plan. (Half the money from Miuraya would have to be repaid; the rest was theirs.) Money is like a snowball. Once you have capital firmly in hand, money breeds money, the way a snowball gets bigger as it rolls along.

Jūzaburō then went to Tokuheiji with an issue that had been weighing on his mind. "I think it's time I told my birth family, the Asanoya, about our plan and asked for their support."

"Yes, now's the time. The sooner the better."

Easy enough for Tokuheiji to say, but for Jūzaburō, who had been put up for adoption, the matter was difficult to broach. His real family was the leading merchant household in Yoshioka. If he could get them to contribute, the project would leap forward. But he was uneasy because on occasional visits, when talking to his brother Jinnai, his nephew Shūemon, or his aged mother, if he mentioned saving Yoshioka, for some reason they all clammed up. He couldn't understand it. In time, he'd stopped making any reference to the project—one that could, after all, endanger the family business.

On April 13, a memorial service was held for Jūzaburō's late father. He had actually died on December 13, but the end of the year was so hectic that they'd chosen to remember him in the spring instead. On the day of the service, Jūzaburō worked up his nerve and went to the house with Tokuheiji in tow, determined to lay out the plan and ask for the family's support.

But when he tried to talk about it, the words wouldn't come. He felt suddenly estranged from them all. Even so, he plowed on. The *Kokuonki* records his first words: "My heart is with you today." He talked for all he was worth. He explained all that the organizers had been through, showed them the promissory note from Miuraya, and said that finally they had high hopes of raising the full sum. The more he talked, the quieter they all were. He ended with these words: "I would like to receive a contribution from this family, too."

Silence enveloped each one there. After a while a voice said, "Who would have thought it? He's exactly like Father!" The speaker was Jinnai. "Listen, Jūzaburō. There's something we never told you."

"What's that?"

"Since you were adopted out of the family, we kept this as our secret and never breathed a word of it to you, but now there's no more need for secrecy. I'll tell you. Our father made a statement on his deathbed."

"What did he say?"

"In his dying hour, he summoned everyone to his bedside and told us, 'My end is coming. As I have often said, I want you to ensure that someone will carry on the family business. Beyond that, as far as you are able, help the poor and the lonely. Take care of your mother. I have no regret on coming to the end of my life, but from my middle years I've had one strong wish. I wanted to put in a request that Yoshioka also receive a subsidy. I'd hoped that the daimyo would reach out to save our town in my lifetime, but life is brief and there is nothing any of us can do about it. Unfortunately, I won't live to see that happen. I ask you not to use the money I saved for any other purpose. Since I was unable to achieve my purpose, then you do it, my son—and if you can't, then let it be my grandson, Shūemon, who does it. However many generations it takes, never forget this high goal. Use my money to ensure the survival and prosperity of Yoshioka.' Then he gripped my hand and seemed ready to breathe his last. With all my heart I said, 'Father, I have heard your dying wish. I too will put away money year by year and watch for the right time. If I fail, then I will tell Shūemon. We will carry out your wish, I promise you.' After that he didn't speak again, but he nodded, and died smiling."

"No one ever told me any of this!" Jūzaburō exclaimed, tears welling.

Never did he dream that his father and he had come up with the same idea for saving the town. His brother's next words surprised him even more.

"I talked it over with Mother and we agreed not to tell you. We thought that was for the best. For all we knew, our fortune might be endangered, and we didn't want to involve you in our financial difficulties. Mother and I share Father's feelings completely. We are prepared to use all our family goods to save Yoshioka. But you are truly your father's son—without ever having been told any of this, you did your utmost to secure the town's future, even to the point of being willing to bankrupt the Kokudaya family. I don't know what to say. This is the best news you could have given us."

Everyone was in tears, even Tokuheiji.

Red-eyed, Jinnai said, "Today is Father's memorial day, too. I couldn't help breaking down. Now I leave it up to you. How much should we contribute?"

"For now, please let me have your written pledge for five hundred kammon."

"I can only think that Father's desire must have communicated itself to you from beyond the grave. I want to say a prayer to Father before his memorial tablet and tell Mother, so wait a moment."

Their mother bustled out and told Jinnai in a scolding voice, "You don't have to wait for anything. Hurry up and write out the paper these men came for!"

Jinnai laid writing things in front of the memorial tablet in the family shrine, and then carefully wrote out a pledge for five hundred kammon, more than a tenth of the capital needed, and handed it to Jūzaburō and Tokuheiji.

The following day brought an even bigger surprise. First Tokuheiji called on Jinnai to express his appreciation. While there, he hardened his heart and said: "Thank you for what you did yesterday. At this point, we have the five hundred ryō from Miuraya plus your five hundred kammon. But it's still far from enough. I realize this is asking a lot, but would you make a larger contribution?"

Ordinarily, such a boldfaced request would be met with anger. But Jinnai said simply, "I'll double the amount. Add on another five hundred." He even indicated willingness to give more if necessary—but any more than that and Tokuheiji knew the family would go out of business.

"No," he said. "If you would kindly raise the amount to one thousand kammon, that would be enough." And he went home.

Bit by bit, the money was coming together. But even in their group, deep down some were reluctant to make any donation, and in time a few of them voiced their biggest concern: "What if Miuraya Sōemon turns out to be dishonorable and doesn't cough up the money after all? Then our plan goes up in smoke."

"If that happens," Tokuheiji said, "Jūzaburō, Jūbei, and I will raise the money, even if we have to go naked and sell ourselves into bondage. We've said that all along." He then produced the oath written on crow-paper and slapped it on the floor.

His vehemence silenced the grumbling. The others quickly assured him they understood and shared his commitment, but Tokuheiji didn't ease up. "Then where this plan is concerned, none of you will act dishonorably, either. Is that right?" Confronted in this way, the men had to agree. Everyone nodded.

Watching, Jūzaburō marveled. Tokuheiji had turned the ripple of dissension on its head, using it to create solidarity and renew everyone's sense of purpose. It had all happened in the space of an instant.

The next hurdle was to make the appeal to Lord Shigemura. Would it work? Was it in fact possible for them to lend him money and in return receive interest and have their tax burden decreased? Jūzaburō finally asked Tokuheiji the question that had been eating at him.

"It looks like we'll have the necessary money in hand. But how do we persuade the daimyo to approve our plan? Just because we submit a petition doesn't mean it will automatically be approved."

"I have an idea."

"What is it?"

"Do you know Ōtomo Gunji?"

"Ōtomo of the Tadaki clan? I know him by name."

"Good. Then you'll agree that he would know better than anyone in Yoshioka how Lord Shigemura is apt to respond."

Ōtomo was a vassal of Yoshioka's feudal lord, Tadaki, Date. They decided to start by talking to him. Together, Tokuheiji and Jūzaburō set off for his house.

Yoshioka wasn't just any post town. It was one of the "48 Date strongholds" set up by Date Masamune to get around the prohibition on multiple castles in a domain. Because Yoshioka was designed like a castle town, its roads were winding and hilly. People commonly referred to the "seven twists and eight hills" of Yoshioka. Another nickname was "loincloth town," a reference to a loincloth's many folds and twists. To guard against enemy attack, the roads turned at right angles periodically, so you walked and walked without progressing very far. At intervals the neighborhood name changed, from Hightown to Middletown to Lowtown.

The two men set out on a "loincloth" journey, navigating the twisting roads all the way to Lowtown, where Ōtomo lived. Tadaki's residence was surrounded by samurai homes. Ōtomo was far poorer than Jūzaburō, but in keeping with his samurai status his house had a small gate. He also observed samurai etiquette in talking to them, sitting across a threshold from them and at a slightly higher elevation.

When they had outlined their plan, Ōtomo sighed. "What a devil of an idea you've come up with! And why come here to tell me about it?"

"We're wondering if, supposing we were able to present this idea, his lordship would give it serious consideration. We came to sound you out on the likelihood of that happening. Also, what would be the best way to increase the chances of his agreeing to our proposal? We want your guidance on these matters."

Ōtomo looked thoughtful. "No telling what will happen unless you try."

"Sir, this is the only request we will ever make of you. Would you please ask around at the government office you frequent?"

He frowned. "I'll think about it."

Jūzaburō and Tokuheiji trudged home.

Soon after that a message came from Ōtomo: "I have looked into the matter you brought up the other day, so come back." The two men gladly retraced their steps down the twisting roads.

Unlike last time, now he was talkative. He apparently had the conscientious spirit of a true bureaucrat and once assigned a task could not rest until it was done. After they left the other day, he had sat down and written to a government official he knew and had also kept his eyes and ears open.

For Jūzaburō, this was the first he had ever heard of how samurai government worked.

"In a government office," said Ōtomo, "what matters most is precedent."

Samurai government operated on the "let sleeping dogs lie" principle. The domain's approach was passive, so unless villages put in requests, no new business was ever done. If commoners requested something new, officials examined precedents to see if there was anything similar, and made inquiries. In Sendai this was the job of an official in the Finance Ministry with the title "financial investigator." For important projects, the financial investigator consulted with the district headman, comparing cases and seeking to avoid inequality.

This emphasis on precedent and examining past instructions was nothing new. It began with officials administering the *ritsuryō* codes of ancient times and was further developed by lawyers in the bureaucracy of the Kamakura and Muromachi shogunates. In the Edo period, domain government was based decisively on adherence to precedent. Administrative records piled up in domain archives with an astounding number of tags attached, along with tables of contents for easy reference. By the time of the feudal domains in Japan's early modern period, this system of government was firmly entrenched.

"Now then," said Ōtomo. "About your case..."

"What did you find out?"

"There's a strong difference of opinion, and it's hard to tell which way it may go. Some officials praised the request, saying it has no parallel in history. Never before have the people been so united in a request, they said. They'd never seen or heard of such a thing in any domain annals. They thought if you made a formal presentation, his lordship would be certain to take it up. However..."

The two men's faces clouded over.

"Go on," said Jūzaburō.

"Others said the plan was too high-minded and that that would actually work against it. One official said, that if it passed, the common people would be the ones acting nobly, and the domain would seem to be poorly run. He thought this might come across as malevolent. Petitioners whose intentions are too high-minded stand less of a chance, he said."

They were horrified. This was the worst outcome they could have imagined. For long years, Sendai Domain had imposed all the taxes it wished on Yoshioka, providing no aid whatever. It was as if the domain sought to annihilate them. The domain was in the wrong. Long-suffering residents of Yoshioka had finally joined together and scraped up money they didn't have, not out of self-interest but as a way of forging a path forward for the town. Now they were told that some government officials were of the opinion that what they were trying to do was "too high-minded"—that it would only call attention to the domain's remissness and was apparently designed to make the authorities look bad.

The daimyo and senior officials were entirely too self-centered, Jūzaburō thought, aggrieved.

Ōtomo went on, "Others pointed out that this proposal isn't in the domain's long-term interest. If you lowered the interest rate by a considerable amount, given that your aim is laudable, permission might be granted."

Poppycock.

If you borrowed money, interest accrued on the loan at a standard rate. This was common sense. But apparently the domain had no intention of paying interest at standard rates. They saw interest as somehow disadvantageous and were willing to cooperate on the condition that the interest be kept low—ideas without a shred of pity or decency.

"So basically," said Tokuheiji on the way home, "we still don't know what to expect."

"We never thought this would be easy," said Jūzaburō. "Let's keep going and not lose heart." What else was there to say?

Not all the news was gloomy. Having found ways to raise the money they needed, Jūzaburō and the others met periodically in Kichijōin, a temple in the center of town where townsmen often got together.

At one such meeting, something wonderful happened. It started when a participant voiced this concern: "One thing bothers me. We're borrowing money from Miuraya to raise the thousand ryō we need to move our plan forward. So even if we start earning a hundred ryō in annual interest, for the first few years we'll need to use that money to pay him back. But the people of

Yoshioka think they're coming into money right away. When that doesn't happen, and the money goes instead to a rich Sendai merchant, they're bound to be upset and accuse us of fraud and embezzlement. We'll be hauled into court. Our plan will be ruined."

The speaker had a point. Jūzaburō and the others present were fairly well educated, but not everybody in town was. There was genuine apprehension over how the illiterate townsfolk might react. However, just as they were discussing this situation, voices rang out.

"Gentlemen! Don't you worry yourselves about a thing like that!"

"We'd never say any such thing, please believe it!"

The voices belonged to Dengorō of Middletown and Heihachi of Lowtown, men who worked in the temple kitchen. They were emphatic. "Maybe we can't pitch in money to help your plan, but we can surely tell the trouble you're going to for us all. Nobody gets the money they've got coming till after Miuraya gets his back, is that right? We'll go door to door and make sure everybody gets that straight. We'll get folks to sign a statement promising not to make any rash accusations."

At the men's eagerness to help out by going among the farmers and getting them to sign a covenant, Jūzaburō felt his eyes moisten.

The Edo period, particularly the latter half, from the late eighteenth to the mid-nineteenth century, was a time when the common folk of Japan shone. They displayed a level of kindness and decency rarely seen in any civilized society. The average person was of a moral rectitude unusual in any era. Heihachi was such a man. He owned no land to speak of and lived in a tiny house in Lowtown, eking out a living by working as a temple handyman, doing things like carrying meals to memorial services and sweeping up in front of the temple gate.

How much say a person had in Edo society depended on whether he was a landowner or not; those who were landless were not recognized within their village community as *ikkenmae* (meaning a house that held rights and duties) or invited to town meetings. Someone like Heihachi therefore had no responsibility in town affairs. Yet even he began running around—running riot, you could almost say—determined to do what he could. "If we don't act, Yoshioka's done for!" This fear filled his heart to bursting. If they didn't get enough money to save the town, there would be no tomorrow. The funny thing was, he took it on himself to visit the wealthy people in town, delivering impassioned speeches to try to raise more money. Jūzaburō and Tokuheiji had already made the rounds and gathered eight contributors. Heihachi made it his goal to find a ninth. Jūzaburō and Tokuheiji knew nothing about his endeavors, and when they eventually found out, they were staggered.

Heihachi's association with the temple meant he had many acquaintances. Moreover, he was used to soliciting temple donations. No one was better than him at collecting money, temple solicitation book in hand. Now he began by calling on Hayasakaya Shinshirō, a sake brewer doing a flourishing business. All the wealthier merchants lived in Hightown; Hayasakaya's was the lone brewery in Lowtown. The family temple was also different. The old-established merchant families had family graves at Kuhonji Temple, but Shinshirō, a relative newcomer, was affiliated with Chūkōji Temple. That explained why he was rather distant from Jūzaburō and Tokuheiji and so had not yet been tapped to join the band of contributors.

Hayasakaya Shinshirō was a forty-year-old man of unmistakable intelligence. An enterprising and active businessman, he soon owned a number of breweries. Lately he had even been heard to say he wanted to excavate for a hot spring, and he could often be seen hiking in the nearby hills, looking for a likely spot.

Heihachi set out to win him over. The *Kokuonki* recounts the episode in its entirety. Heihachi's exact words are recorded, a rarity even for this era when so many records were made for posterity. It is a superb source, affording us a window into the mind of a common man of that day.

"As I am sure you have already heard…"

As Jūzaburō would later learn, Heihachi began with these words and went on talking persuasively at great length. He told Shinshirō straight out how hard the contributors were working. "The gentlemen of Hightown are great men." All the rich residents of Hightown were contributing to the raising of capital, he stressed. Even Jinnai's wife supported the plan; why, it was enough to bring tears to the eyes. Kokudaya Zempachi, who really wasn't very wealthy, had pledged two hundred kammon, becoming the eighth contributor. These fine gentlemen were giving their all to save the three neighborhoods of Yoshioka. When had there ever been such a display of kindness and sincerity? Compared with them, he said, the well-off residents of Lowtown were a disgrace. Since all the contributors were from Hightown, Heihachi and the other Lowtown resident were set to collect interest without having put a penny of their own money into the project.

It is most interesting, and typical of Edo-period commoners, that they weren't attracted by the prospect of a free ride—far from it.

"That would affect the honor of Lowtown residents," said Heihachi. "The folks in Hightown, even those who contributed nothing, would strut around like the town saviors, and we in Lowtown wouldn't be able to hold our heads high. We wouldn't want that to happen, would we?"

During the Edo period, everyone, including commoners, was concerned with "face." This national trait had already been noted in the previous era by European missionaries. It was to avoid losing face that Heihachi sought desperately to persuade the richest man in his neighborhood to loosen his purse strings. He spoke from the heart. "If I could, I'd give money myself, only someone like me hasn't got the wherewithal. But you do. You've got many times more money than I'll ever have. Wouldn't you like to be one of the contributors?" When Shinshirō said nothing, he added, "Your name would go down in history. You really should do it."

Overpowered, finally Shinshirō asked, "How much should I give?"

Heihachi's response is interesting. He folded his arms and said, sounding almost as if he were the brewery owner, "Well, let me see. A man of your standing should give five or six hundred kammon. If you didn't give that much, I doubt if they'd let you in anyway. After all, the rest of them have put up all they own—house and possessions, clothes, even wife and child. Asanoya-san got rid of all his kimono, they say, and owns nothing but the clothes on his back. There's no use committing yourself unless you're ready to give till it hurts. You'll have to give about that much if you want credit for doing all you can as a man of your position."

For Shinshirō, this demand was utterly unreasonable. If he gave five or six hundred kammon, his business would shrivel. He might not have to close up shop, but even so, it wasn't a suggestion he could stomach. Yet on being told that a donation of that size represented "all he could do as a man of his position," he couldn't turn Heihachi down pointblank, either.

More than at any other time in Japanese history, Edo-period society was propped up by the notion of *mibun sōō*: "befitting one's position or social status." Everyone had a given status and was expected to conduct himself accordingly. Ieyasu, founder of the Tokugawa regime, had liked to say "Miso should have the flavor of miso, samurai the flavor of samurai." In other words, everyone should act in a manner appropriate to his station. A samurai's act of ritual disembowelment and a town headman's self-sacrifice to protect villagers were both based on this premise of behaving in accordance with one's station in life. *Mibun sōō* was the most influential social principle of the time. People complied with these conventions as a matter of course; anyone failing to do so was reviled.

Shinshirō would have to make a donation in keeping with his social station. Members of all levels of society would expect no less of him. People in the upper class were particularly put upon in the Edo period, constantly subjected to the common people's merciless injunction to "act in a manner befitting your position." That was what enabled Heihachi to put unrelenting pressure on Shinshirō now.

Shinshirō seemed at a loss. He mumbled, "I know what you're saying…I just don't have the money…please understand."

But Heihachi wasn't about to let him off the hook. By the standards of the day, right was clearly on his side. He proceeded to deliver a sermon on morality.

"Now, sir, that statement is lacking in sincerity. Just think it over. Your family won't prosper forever. Sōzaemon and Rokuzaemon used to have sake shops in this neighborhood, and they enjoyed a good life, but what happened? They and their shops are gone without a trace. It's different if you donate a bell or a statue to a temple. In Middletown, Takaya Gorōshichi and Fukudaya Matasaku both died, but their names live on as temple donors. Just as everyone must die, so riches and poverty are fleeting."

Shinshirō listened in silence.

"The same is true of Akechi Mitsuhide." Wherever Heihachi had picked up this smattering of knowledge, he now expanded on a historical theme. "Akechi caused the death of his own master, General Oda Nobunaga, and was branded a traitor and a murderer. But because he didn't impose land taxes on tenant farmers in Kyoto and gave money toward a bathhouse for the Zen temple Myōshinji, to this day, every time the monks take a bath they read a sutra and light incense on his behalf. Some folks in Kyoto still keep a memorial tablet to him, they say. Why not take these examples to heart and do a good deed that will inspire people in coming generations to honor you? A tiger dies and leaves behind its pelt, a man dies and leaves behind his name. I'm telling you this for your own good. You ought to join the folks who are donating money for this cause. Your good name will live on after you are gone. That can only benefit your descendants in coming generations."

Despite this heartfelt plea, Shinshirō remained silent. He closed his eyes for a bit and seemed to be struggling to come up with some sort of response. Finally, with evident difficulty, he said, "I think I could manage two or three hundred kammon. Five or six hundred is out of the question. Not a cent more than three hundred. Please understand."

And so Hayasakaya Shinshirō became the ninth donor.

Japanese people in the Edo period had a strong sense of public duty. A sense of responsibility permeated all levels of society. People felt, "If I did such-and-such a thing, I'd never be able to face my ancestors. If I don't do the right thing now, I can never make it up to my children and grandchildren." Heihachi had appealed to that sense of obligation to win Shinshirō's consent.

For Jūzaburō and the rest, the news was welcome.

"But some people just wouldn't cough up any money, no matter what I said," Heihachi added sadly.

"Who else did you talk to?" Jūzaburō sounded worried.

Heihachi launched into a detailed account of all those he had failed to convince. Nobody in Middletown was a donor. Thinking that wouldn't do, he had sent Dengorō and another man, Kōemon, to talk to three likely prospects, but all three had turned a deaf ear.

The first was notoriously one of the most tight-fisted men in Yoshioka. Whatever they said, he responded, "That's all well and good, and I'd certainly like to help, but I just haven't got that kind of money." He and they had ended up glaring at one another in silence and parted on bad terms.

The second was a different matter. His business hadn't been doing well in recent years. "I'm secretly envious of those petitioning the daimyo. I suppose I could manage ten or twenty kammon." Judging his case hopeless, they had given up trying.

With the third man too they'd had no luck. "Making a donation would ensure your descendants' longevity," they had assured him, but he still wouldn't give a favorable reply. They thought one hundred kammon would be an appropriate donation, but he refused to negotiate. "Be glad you were born in this difficult time as that will lead to great happiness. Think of your children and grandchildren, and for their sakes do the right thing." Heihachi too had tried his best, he said, but it was no use.

At this time Japanese of every level of society, including commoners, were devotees of what might be called a national religion: family consciousness. This quasi-religion, which was deeply engrained in the residents of Yoshioka, placed supreme value on family continuity and the prosperity of future generations. Along with worship of ancestors (who were commonly referred to as *hotoke*, "Buddha"), worship of descendants was a mainstay of people's thinking. There was extreme fear of having the family line die out, leaving no one to tend to the ancestral graves. In the past, few graves bore individual names and family cemetery plots were rare; but from the Edo period on, the question of who would tend the family grave loomed large in people's minds, and maintaining descendants to perform this task became an overriding goal. Given the choice between what would benefit oneself in this life and what would benefit one's descendants in coming generations, most people would have chosen the latter. Anyone who stated, as one of the unwilling Middletown prospects had done, "If my generation goes under, there won't be any children or grandchildren," was clearly a heretic living only for the moment.

The three merchants who declined to participate were later subjected to harsh criticism by their neighbors. One resisted the appeal largely because Dengorō and Kōemon did an inept job of persuading him, but people held him in scorn forever after: "A born tightwad, and no talent." The hostility became so rampant that a local priest had to step in and try to calm people down: "Now, don't be so antagonistic."

Jūzaburō sighed. Things had come to a pretty pass. He'd sought donations out of the purest of motives, but now donors were being accorded excess respect, and those who couldn't donate were beginning to be looked at askance.

The one most troubled by this development was the district headman, Chisaka Chūnai. As he was responsible for the entire county, he felt compelled to do something. He summoned the other eight contributors and told them, "We have to be discreet."

He went on to explain why. Yoshioka residents were beginning to treat the nine of them with as much awe and deference as if they had been among the forty-seven *rōnin* who famously avenged their master's honor. Others who had contributed nothing were being reviled. Those living in a small world are susceptible to envy and jealousy, and the small world of Yoshioka was already showing signs of division. Each of the nine had put up money from the purest of motives, but not everyone was happy about their action. They needed to be careful, Chūnai said, and proceeded to spell out what he meant.

"However you are treated, put up with it. Avoid traveling far, even on business. Take care not to get sick, and see a doctor at the first sign of illness. Don't say a word about the plan to revive Yoshioka, even if someone asks."

He had a dozen or more pieces of such cautionary advice. All this Jūzaburō and Tokuheiji fully understood. Then he started talking about what would happen if their request was approved. This they were not prepared for.

"There's something that each of us must pass on to our descendants."

"What?"

"I doubt if any of us would boast about it if our plan succeeded, but with future generations there's no telling."

This was true. If Yoshioka were saved by this plan, the nine donors would be feted. Inevitably, that would translate into higher status for their families. Their nine families were sure to acquire lasting prestige in the small community.

"So I want each of you to promise that neither you nor any of your descendants will ever sit in a place of honor."

They took this in. Jūzaburō was saying that from now on, at a drinking party or a town meeting they must be content with the lowest seats. This seemed going a bit far, but no one protested. Each of the eight men, pressed for an answer by Chūnai, answered "No objection." Everyone seemed to accept the injunction as natural. They decided to sign a statement that even if their plan succeeded, their descendants were never to give themselves airs on that account. Chūnai said that they couldn't rest easy without putting it on paper, so that's what they did. Town elders were always getting them to sign statements for self-protection, so they were used to the procedure and willingly complied.

They drew up a number of articles that they called "points of self-restraint," and every man signed it. Jūzaburō wrote out his name as "Kokudaya Jūzaburō" and then sealed it with his blood. Below this he wrote his name in a stylized monogram, feeling like a samurai. The others also each had a monogram, and they appended theirs like samurai also.

Only Shinshirō of the Hayasakaya apparently had no such monogram, or perhaps he took inordinate pride in his shop; in any case, he drew out his shop seal from his pouch and affixed it to the paper. Now the circle of names was complete.

They thought this would be all the paperwork necessary, but they were wrong.

"After we present our proposal to the daimyo," said Chūnai with a worried air, "if even one of us backs off, the entire scheme will collapse."

The men exchanged looks. They had faith in one another, but it was true—if even one person reneged, it would mean disaster.

"Then why not have each of us write out a note declaring our intentions?" Who made this suggestion isn't clear from the record, but someone in the group did.

As an aside, it was rare at this time in Japan's history for peasants starting a movement of any kind to leave a record of individual resolve. Usually before an uprising or a petition, the group's intention would be expressed in a single statement that everyone signed. In that sense, these nine men of Yoshioka were unconventional. As modern people might do, they each declared their individual intent to save Yoshioka and committed it to writing.

Chūnai himself was the first to take up the brush. "If by any chance some misunderstanding should arise concerning money, to pay what is owed I pledge to sell not only my house and land, my possessions, and my clothing, but also my wife and children. My family and I are prepared to stand by this pledge."

Next, town headman Ikuemon wrote: "I have come to this resolution after earnest discussion with my mother, who is of the main branch of the house of Asanoya. Even if I have to wear a sack over my head and go begging, I will have no regrets. I have the same resolve regarding my son Tōkichi."

Jūzaburō decided to write exactly how he felt. "I am ready to sell myself into bondage if that is what it takes."

A farmer's greatest fear was becoming a *mutaka no mizunomi*, a "landless water-drinking peasant," i.e. someone who rented land from tenant farmers. This is what selling oneself into bondage meant. Only those who paid their annual land tax and were entitled to work the land were considered fully human. Those who had lost their house and land had no choice but to sell themselves into indentured servitude to avoid starving while paying back what they owed. The family would be broken up. Children would be pushed around their whole lives and could never marry. For *ombyakushō*, "farmers of the domain," second in status only to samurai, being sold into bondage was a living death sentence.

The moment Jūzaburō wrote out the fate he feared most, the face of his son, Otoemon, rose in his mind. Otoemon's life would be ruined, all because he had been adopted into the Kokudaya family. Far from his expectation of a peaceful future as master of the family sake shop, thanks to Jūzaburō he might end up in bondage. And yet there was no turning back.

Pulling himself together, Jūzaburō added, "My son Otoemon also says that whatever tribulations may lie ahead, he pledges on his life that he will see this plan through."

What would Tokuheiji, sitting next to him, write? Jūzaburō peered curiously at the page. Lo and behold, unlike everyone else, he was going on about his wife. Jūzaburō stifled laughter. "When I asked my wife, she said, 'I figured you were thinking about something like that. Women in all ages have followed their husband's lead; that's nothing I need to make a fresh resolution about. From the day I married you, my life has been in your hands. So do as you think best.'"

Tokuheiji's wife Natsu was around twenty-four or twenty-five years old. After spending his youth cultivating tea, he had married late, well into his thirties, and his wife was some fifteen years younger than him. Natsu was a beautiful woman with clear, fair skin. Since marrying, Tokuheiji had done a complete turnabout. Once a misogynist, he now doted on his young wife and could hardly bear to be away from her for a day. He was the most brilliant man in town, and she had him wrapped firmly around her little finger.

So Tokuheiji, a man of rigorous logic, had merely quoted his wife, whose opinion amounted to "Suit yourself." Jūzaburō found it amusing.

Once they had all written out their pledges and assembled them, they were ready to take their case to the daimyo.

Suddenly there was a loud pounding on the door. Everyone jumped. Here they were engaged in secret talks about a petition to the domain. Had word leaked out? Had someone come to arrest them?

But no. When the door opened, who should appear but Heihachi and his friends, those men who had bent over backwards to help raise funds. Attired in thin, grubby kimono despite the harsh winter winds, they turned their meek eyes to the men inside. "We came to ask you a favor," said Heihachi. They wanted the petition read aloud to the entire town on the night of the twenty-third, when it was customary for everyone to gather at one of the local temples to await the rising of the last-quarter moon; people would confine themselves in the temple until dawn, offering prayers of supplication. Would Jūzaburō and the rest come and let everyone know the contents of the petition?

At this time in history, when any political gathering might be regarded as an uprising, villagers were at least allowed to gather at night to drink together and celebrate the moonrise and sunrise. This was a custom they themselves had come up with.

There was a "read-aloud" political culture at the time. As is often portrayed in historical dramas, notice boards would contain simple injunctions like "Obey the law," "Christianity is forbidden," "No gambling." The daily stream of laws issued by the domain did not appear on notice boards. High as Japan's literacy rate was in comparison to some other countries, more than half the general population was illiterate. Reading aloud therefore played an important role in Edo-period laws and politics, particularly in the seventeenth century. The town headman or other leader would assemble everyone in one place and read aloud the laws and regulations, thus extending the feudal lord's domination to every last resident. Not until around the beginning of the twentieth century would awareness of laws be disseminated routinely through official gazettes and newspapers, i.e. the written word.

On the night of the twenty-third, the town of Yoshioka was enveloped in a peculiar mood. This time the mood was not festive; every person in town walked silently in the dark to the temple. The crowd of people anxious to hear this news that would deeply affect each of them swelled into the compound, filling it to capacity.

Jūzaburō trembled to think that the fate of the town hung on what would now happen. The air was thick with tension as he and the other eight began slowly to read the petition aloud to the gathered throng.

Of the 219 households in Yoshioka, sixteen have gone bankrupt. The town is poor; only eight or nine people own land valued above one kammon. The markets held every five days allow people to supplement their incomes, but such business is declining. If the town is to continue supplying post horses for his lordship's use, something must be done: we request that taxes be reduced by six kammon per year for landowners and four kammon per year for landless homeowners. However, we do not ask his lordship to grant this request for nothing. We pledge to give him 4,500 kammon by the coming year, when he next leads a procession to Edo for his obligatory residence, and another 1,500 kammon three years later at the time of the following one, for a total of 6,000 kammon. In return, we ask for the above tax exemptions.

The plan would never work unless the entire town backed it as one. They explained the petition in simple language. It asked for a reduction in yearly household taxes while guaranteeing the daimyo 6,000 kammon in two unequal payments over a four-year period.

The crowd listened in silence. No one so much as coughed. Everyone understood the momentousness of the matter. Midway through the reading came the clanging of an alarm bell, signaling a fire in a neighboring village. Even then, nobody made a sound or even stood up. They all continued to listen solemnly.

On the way home, Tokuheiji turned to Jūzaburō and said, "Even though there was a fire, no one got up to go. I'll never forget the intensity of their expressions."

Encroaching poverty was more frightening to the townspeople than fire, Jūzaburō thought.

The day they submitted the petition to the daimyo was truly a red-letter day for Yoshioka. Everyone prayed earnestly for the success of the petition. Three loads of sake were delivered to Jūzaburō and the rest, and the whole town insisted on seeing them off. Jūzaburō had wanted a quiet send-off, but this was not the case.

Young men seemed bent on tagging along all the way to Sendai. But if too many people turned out, the daimyo might get the wrong idea and assume this was a *gōso*, an illegal collective petition by peasants to those in power.

Edo society had communal associations known as *goningumi*, "five-household groups," consisting of homeowners and landlords who answered to the neighborhood chief. For the send-off, Tokuheiji urged the townspeople to have only the appointed leader of each group see them off, but no one paid any attention. The group leaders followed the nine on their journey and intoned prayers. The people's hopes and desires clung fast to the band of petitioners as they set off.

Petitions were handled by the magistrate's office. Jūzaburō and the rest headed for the office of Kurokawa County, which had jurisdiction over Yoshioka. All nine petitioners, including Chisaka Chūnai, were officially farmers, and anything they submitted to the domain required a prefatory note from the magistrate. Yashima Dennosuke, the magistrate on duty that month, was an ordinary official who, like most of his ilk, looked with disfavor on irregular petitions. When at length the nine finally managed to meet him, he treated them slightingly and barely glanced at their petition before saying with a wooden stare, "See Hashimoto Gon'emon. He's the one you need to talk to."

In other words, Yashima wanted nothing to do with it and was fobbing them off on the off-duty magistrate who shared his post. A clear evasion of responsibility. Tokuheiji was grim-faced. Probably to an official anxious to avoid rocking the boat, having to deal with an unprecedented petition that fit into no neat category and send it up to one's superior was annoying. And yet the petition couldn't be dismissed outright, since it bore the signature of the district headman. "I'll foist it on Hashimoto." This was Yashima's ploy.

So began a time of endless waffling and red tape.

More than at any time previously, bureaucratic red tape was oppressively complex. Few societies in the world can have afflicted people with such onerous paperwork. A main reason was that during that time of extended peace, there were too many samurai and no battles for them to fight. In the late sixteenth century, the small island country of Japan had been overrun with warriors. The number peaked around Hideyoshi's Korean invasions of 1592 and 1597, when out of a population of twelve or thirteen million, half a million were samurai—and if their families were included, the samurai class numbered easily over a million. Then in the peaceful Edo era, Japan was saddled with a bloated population of idle samurai. Jobs that could have been done by a single man were assigned to two or more so that all could have work. Moreover, they worked on a monthly rotating schedule; this was believed necessary to keep any one person from having a preponderance of power. In samurai society, standing out from one's fellows and making a show of authority were shunned. The exercise of arbitrary power by anyone but one's lord was unpardonable. To prevent this from happening, samurai made group decisions and took group action.

Samurai government was run by officials with extremely limited authority. Who actually made decisions was never very clear; obfuscation of authority was the whole idea. Any kind of administrative decision followed a complicated route involving documents sent hither and yon to be stamped by an inordinate number of officials.

Back to our story.

Take it to Hashimoto Gon'emon, Yashima had ordered. While they hadn't expected the way to be smooth, the nine felt crushed. The order was particularly hard on them since Hashimoto was far away in the Nakaniida district office, separated from Yoshioka by steep terrain. Roads that were execrable to begin with had been washed out in many places by recent rains.

Officials could inflict suffering on commoners without batting an eye, Jūzaburō thought resentfully. Still, frustrating as the order was, there was no way around it.

Negotiations with the domain required the presence of top village officials, so Chūnai and Ikuemon accompanied Tokuheiji on horseback over the bad roads. Jūzaburō was glad that Tokuheiji, the wiser of the two of them, was the one to go; but when he went to see the party off on the morning of their departure, he became a little worried. Tokuheiji's horse looked weak enough to collapse at any moment. Jūzaburō wondered if the animal could make it safely all the way to Nakaniida. "You sure you'll be all right?" he asked.

Tokuheiji replied calmly from the saddle: "Whatever happens, I'll never let go of the petition, not even if I die." He was wearing the precious document slung around his neck.

Jūzaburō's fears proved well grounded, as along the way the horse stumbled in a puddle of muddy water and Tokuheiji was thrown to the ground.

Chūnai ran to help him up, afraid that the petition was now covered in mud. He brushed off the outer wrapping and checked the inside. Not only was the petition safe, but Tokuheiji himself had barely smudged his clothing and was standing upright, unharmed. Surely this was a sign of the protection of Kumano Shrine. All three men rinsed their hands in a roadside pool and offered thanks. Again and again as they traveled through the forests of Michinoku they stumbled, and each time they offered thanks for divine protection.

Finally they arrived at the Nakaniida district office. Now if they were turned away, it was all over; they understood, half resigned to failure. But Hashimoto granted them an audience and also carefully examined the petition while Tokuheiji prostrated himself and prayed.

"Lift your heads," Hashimoto said, and the three men looked up simultaneously. "Never before has there been such a petition!" he declared in a shocked voice.

Instantly, they later said, all three had the same thought: "We're doomed."

Hashimoto's next words took them by surprise: "I will personally see to it that this gets into the right hands."

Wordless emotion flooded through them. The magistrate's warm words continued. He was smiling cheerfully, the way people do when they're truly glad. Then, to their further astonishment, he suggested that the four of them share a drink. Modest refreshments were brought out—sake and some soup. He praised the three men's resolve. After an evening of hospitality, they stumbled tipsily back to their lodgings, only to be surprised again when soon after they arrived a messenger came, bearing an invitation for them all to return in the morning for breakfast. They were awestruck. Never had they heard of a magistrate according farmers such a reception.

"We are farmers. Please remind him of this and permit us to decline his invitation."

"Don't worry," said the messenger. "He said to tell you it's because he is so pleased with your action on behalf of other farmers. You needn't hesitate to accept the invitation."

And so in the morning they presented themselves with trepidation. After breakfast, they were shown the note that Hashimoto had written to accompany their petition.

On returning to Yoshioka, they shared all the developments with Jūzaburō. Hashimoto's note, the equivalent of a personal recommendation, guaranteed that the petition would work its way up. Hashimoto had also promised to contact Yashima. "You can count on me," he had said.

Yashima's attitude changed radically. The next time they called on him, he said, "I heard all about this from Hashimoto. This is a very happy turn of events. Your petition is top-notch. Certainly his lordship will never have seen the like of it." He held the petition high over his head and spread it out respectfully.

Jūzaburō remembered something Tokuheiji had once said: "A small-minded bureaucrat never does anything new. All he does is blindly follow others' lead." Apparently it was true. But at least now Yashima had warmed to their cause and things were happening. The end was in sight. Yoshioka would be saved.

But the officials were not so obliging.

The news came out of the blue. It was January 8, the day after the Festival of Spring Herbs, when everyone ate rice gruel flavored with seven wild herbs. "Come quickly." Chisaka Chūnai sent out this message. Intuitively, Tokuheiji knew this was it, the word they had been waiting for. They had submitted the petition at the end of November, so a month and a half had gone by. The time had come.

Domain offices dealt quickly with ordinary requests. The response to an unprecedented petition, however, could be a desperately long time in coming. The men understood this, but they had still hoped for an answer before the year was out. The domain customarily cleared its docket at the end of the year, so the pace of work quickened. Hoping this would work to their advantage, they had waited hopefully, but time came to put up New Year's pine decorations and still there was no word.

Until around the Genroku era (1688–1704), daimyo were not so slow in handling official business. Before that, daimyo clans still functioned along the lines of military organizations, briskly efficient with little red tape. Officials relied less on legal codes and more on their own discretion. But as the long peace stretched on, things changed. The number of officials in the domain administrative structure ballooned and communication degenerated.

Even if the daimyo made a swift decision, notification had to descend through the ranks, from comptroller to country magistrate to magistrate to the district headman. Tokuheiji had been expecting no news until the New Year, and then came the message from Chūnai. His gut told him what it meant.

Chūnai's house was a little removed from the center of town. Although a large, imposing structure, it differed considerably in appearance from a samurai residence, as covered ceilings and cross-beams were forbidden to non-samurai.

Sendai Domain was particularly strict about such things. Not even Chūnai, despite his important position in the community, was allowed a ceiling. However, his family was granted a different, important mark of status: in all of Yoshioka, they alone were allowed to use umbrellas. Everyone else had to be satisfied with raincoats of oilpaper or straw. At the entrance to Chūnai's house stood a rare sight in this area, a line of umbrellas.

Tokuheiji was ushered past them into an inner room where Chūnai sat in the seat of honor. The first words he spoke were, "I'm very sorry."

Tokuheiji stiffened. Had their petition been denied? He felt as if he were in a bad dream, but the district headman's words sounded clearly in his ears.

"The petition came back with a note from the daimyo. It's a shame, but our hard work came to nothing. More than one application is often necessary before the daimyo will grant an appeal like this, though, so don't lose heart."

"Let me get this straight. Our petition was rejected?"

Chisaka nodded slowly.

This was awful. Their precious petition had been shunted from official to official and then tossed out.

"Maybe we asked too much of his lordship after all," said Chūnai, as if he were starting to distance himself from the enterprise.

It mustn't end like this, thought Tokuheiji in desperation. "Chisaka-sama, you have to let me see the comment. Would you please show it to me?"

Chūnai unrolled the note and spread it out. Tokuheiji stared.

"Difficult to review." The petition had reached the comptroller, who dismissed it as with these callous words. The note concluded, "For this reason, the case is closed." But there was no reason! The paper might as well have been blank. The response was as contemptuous as it could be. The petitioners had been kept waiting for months, only to be told that the domain could not review their petition.

The biggest flaw in Edo government was the lack of a legislative assembly serving subjects of lower station, such as existed in Europe. There was little recourse for ordinary people to have their appeals quickly received and acted upon. Though there was a sophisticated bureaucracy based on loyalty to one's lord and duty to superiors, government didn't adequately reflect the voice of the people. Tokugawa Yoshimune (1684–1751), the eighth shogun, had installed suggestion boxes, but as time went on these became a mere matter of form, a convention in which his successors showed little interest. Each domain had a suggestion box, but they were used primarily to file anonymous reports of official wrongdoing and were not a reliable way to file administrative petitions. In only one place were appeals from the lower classes consistently reflected in government and a modern system set up with the avowed goal of *fukoku kyōhei*, "rich country, strong army": Kumamoto Domain in southern Japan. If Yoshioka had been a post town there, or in some other region gaining in influence, the appeal might not have been given short shrift. But Yoshioka was in Sendai, and it had been rejected after barely a glance.

Despite this setback, Tokuheiji's response was amazing. "It seems to me," he said finally, "this rejection must be a test of our resolve." Resentment against one's superiors was simply unthinkable. Even a man of Tokuheiji's intellect approached the authorities with implicit trust.

Chūnai looked surprised. "Hmm, that could very well be," he admitted. "But don't you think the petition placed an undue burden on his lordship?" At a time when the daimyo needed funds, the people of Yoshioka had submitted a self-seeking petition; wasn't that why it had been so easily dismissed? Their petition did require the daimyo to divert funds in order to earn money for interest. Chūnai's loyalty lay ultimately with the daimyo, who allowed him and his family the privilege of carrying umbrellas. "Maybe there's a way we can manage without troubling his lordship," he suggested. "What if we diverted the funds ourselves and distributed the interest to the townspeople?"

Furious, Tokuheiji cried out, "Chisaka-sama! Surely you aren't saying we should scrap this petition? If we could possibly divert the funds ourselves and earn interest, do you think we'd have come up with this plan in the first place?"

Yes, for a generation or two it might work, but sooner or later, coming generations were bound to forget what their forebears had done and spend the capital, winding up with nothing. With little industry in the region to speak of, investing the capital profitably would be no easy task. How could they accomplish what the daimyo, with his vast credit, could not? This was Tokuheiji's opinion, and he was undoubtedly right.

"Our petition to save Yoshioka will benefit his lordship," Tokuheiji declared. If things went on as they were, the town would shrivel up and die. With fewer people and post horses, they would be unable to meet his lordship's needs, whereas if Yoshioka thrived, his lordship would have a steady source of land tax and could assign work to the town as he saw fit. There were any number of cases where daimyo had reached out a helping hand to post towns, even without a cash incentive close to what the petitioners were offering. If they reworked the petition and kept submitting it as many times as necessary, eventually the domain would have to come round. As district headman, it was incumbent upon Chisaka to take in their side.

Tokuheiji's words had the ring of logic and truth. Yet Chisaka seemed to be thinking primarily of holding onto his position without offending the governing authorities.

Tokuheiji felt a flare of anger. Until that moment he had never wavered in his respect for the district headman, but this was too much. Trifling honors were all it took to make him fawn on his superiors and turn his back on the sufferings of the people. Not even Chisaka Chūnai, a man known for his integrity, was immune. It saddened Tokuheiji to think that this was the way of the world. What made it worse was that domain officials took advantage of this human weakness, providing village officials with surnames and sometimes swords to win them over. A first-rate official would turn toward the common people and do all he could on their behalf without benefit of such privileges, but people were easily taken in. And as long as this happened, this rotten world would never change. Oh, it made his blood boil!

In that moment, this sake merchant from a Tohoku backwater stumbled on a fresh way of thinking that transcended his time. He saw the significance of power and politics.

"Chisaka-sama, who are you going to work for, them or us?" Tokuheiji pressed the district headman unrelentingly. He didn't care a straw for the man's authority now. He wanted only to convert him. Concentrating on that goal, he kept on reasoning and remonstrating. Since Chūnai was in public office, it was perhaps only to be expected that he would take the side of the authorities. On the other hand, like the other petitioners, he too was a Yoshioka *ombyakushō*, a "peasant of the domain."

Tokuheiji, looking hard at Chūnai, reminded him where his first allegiance lay. "Since the time of Asanoya Jinnai VI, everyone in that family—women and children, too—has been saving copper coins in a jar, hoping against hope to see this dream fulfilled. Even the maids save money for this purpose! Doesn't their sacrifice mean anything to you?" His voice broke with emotion. His eyes were bloodshot. He pleaded with Chūnai till he was hoarse. Finally, the sun rose and a rooster crowed.

Chūnai succumbed. "All right." He tried to sound optimistic: it might be all to the good that the petition had been rejected for no specific reason, he said. The authorities hadn't spelled out any reason for the rejection, which left hope that next time they might listen. "We'll try."

Tokuheiji's determination had won out.

They would of course resubmit the petition. The question was, what to do in the interim? Chūnai and Tokuheiji decided it would be best to keep the rejection secret from the other seven. News that the petition had been denied might cause some to waver. If even one man dropped out, the thousand ryō might recede beyond reach. But that wasn't their only worry. Someone might take the rejection so much to heart that he would run off to Sendai, confront the daimyo procession, and lob a protest letter directly into a senior official's palanquin.

That form of appeal was strictly forbidden. Not only would the offender risk being put to death, but all chance of their plea getting a fair hearing would forever disappear. Letting the truth be known was fraught with danger.

"Even if we try again," Chūnai cautioned, "we'd better wait a while."

"How long?"

"Let's see… If we waited six months, then I don't think they would take it amiss."

"Six months." Tokuheiji sighed. For all that time, they would have to keep the truth hidden. Wasn't that a betrayal of their comrades, who were as anxious as they were to see the plan succeed?

He wanted to share the disappointing news with Jūzaburō right away; but for now, he and Chūnai agreed to keep the others in the dark.

But the they couldn't hide the truth forever.

"This is taking too long!" In April, one member of their group impatiently appealed to the domain office and was told that the plea had long since been turned down. Jūzaburō and the others rushed to Chisaka Chūnai's house.

"Why didn't you tell us?" Jūzaburō wanted to know. "Weren't you holding back a little too much?" Anyone else might have yelled, "How could you be so unfeeling?" Jūzaburō's choice of words would seem to indicate that he himself was a man of considerable reserve.

"We have a secret plan," Chūnai and Tokuheiji insisted. "Leave it to us." If word got out and young men in town took it upon themselves to make a rash appeal to a high official, all would be lost. The two of them would cope, they promised. They just needed time to carry out their hush-hush idea.

What idea was that, the men demanded. The mood turned ugly. At this rate, they would soon get into a shouting match. To prevent a falling-out, Jūzaburō spoke up. "If Sugawaraya Tokuheiji and the district headman say they have a plan, all we can do is trust them and wait."

His words had a calming effect and brought the men to themselves. It was ingrained in the people of Tohoku to follow without question any decisions handed down from on high—a cultural trait shared by Japanese at the other end of the archipelago, in southern Kyushu. Tohoku farming communities had a peculiar docility toward their superiors. Everyone down to the last member would follow the decisions of the village chief. By contrast, villages in the Kinai region around Nara and present-day Kyoto were different. This old-fashioned simplicity was the saving of Chūnai and Tokuheiji.

Although they had announced they had a plan, Chūnai and Tokuheiji were troubled. Would it really be possible to overturn the domain's decision and push through the town's petition?

"Looks like we'll have to rely on Hashimoto after all," murmured Tokuheiji. When they first presented their petition, the magistrate Hashimoto Gon'emon had taken their side. They would go back to him, find out why their petition had been rejected, and then figure out a new approach. After that they could try again. This was Tokuheiji's idea.

But this time, the only one entitled to meet with Hashimoto was Chisaka Chūnai. Tokuheiji, lacking a proper surname, was officially "Farmer Sugawaraya." So it was Chūnai who headed for the magistrate's house, his horse stumbling along mountain roads muddy from the early summer rains. When he finally arrived, he pleaded earnestly with Hashimoto, emphasizing how pitiful the people of Yoshioka would be with their one hope dashed. Fortunately, Hashimoto was a man of understanding who lent a sympathetic ear. His dealings with farmers had made him well aware of their sufferings, though yet why the plight of Yoshioka residents should have touched him so is a mystery. No records survive concerning this magistrate who died in obscurity.

In any case, Chūnai sensed that getting through to Hashimoto was their only hope. Desperation made him eloquent. He recounted the story of old Jinnai and the dream he had long ago. "For the sake of his dream, he reduced his daily intake of food and set aside money in a jar. At first, no one knew why.

Some people laughed at him for being a skinflint. But on his deathbed, Jinnai explained. As he lay dying, he gripped his son's hand and told him, 'I have a dream. I wanted to save up money and present it to the lord of Sendai, and in return gain relief from the tax burden that is suffocating us. I couldn't make it happen in my lifetime. I want you to carry on where I left off.' With these words, he breathed his last. His son took his father's name and began following his example, hoarding coins. This went on for decades. Without telling anyone what he was doing or why, he saved every penny with steadfast determination. Privately, he told his family of his mission to bring Yoshioka out of poverty. Instead of protesting, his entire family, the women included, also began to save money. As word of what they were doing began to spread, others joined in. The result of all this was the petition we submitted, but it came back without a word of explanation. It's deeply disappointing." Chūnai was normally taciturn, but he spoke now with deep urgency.

As he listened, Hashimoto's expression changed, and then he interrupted: "Chisaka, wait. Are you saying that this scheme isn't something you and your associates came up with for the first time?"

"That's right, but why..."

"The point is crucial, so let me ask again. Is this petition something that people in Yoshioka have long had in mind?"

"Yes. Jinnai first thought of it long ago."

Hashimoto registered amazement and then sighed. "In that case something must be done. I'll go and explain the situation to County Magistrate Imaizumi."

Hashimoto, a lowly magistrate, was offering to go to Sendai with the express purpose of overturning high officials' decision against Yoshioka. Chūnai couldn't believe his ears. For a moment he wondered if the man had lost his mind. Yet he seemed perfectly serious.

Hashimoto had already looked into the matter and found out why the officials had given the plea short shrift. They saw it as a shameful attempt to profit from the daimyo's financial difficulties, as if the nine were practicing usury. Hashimoto was willing to go to Sendai himself and clear up the misunderstanding.

Chisaka's administrative experience told him how formidable a challenge this would be. He also knew it was something he himself could never do. To be big-hearted at home, among family and friends, wasn't hard, but once a man joined the domain bureaucracy he grew used to going along with the official position, regardless of his true feelings. He had to kowtow to superiors and couldn't express himself to them the way he would to family and friends. Hope lay in the faint chance of linking hearts. The flame of old Jinnai's resolve had passed to Tokuheiji and from Tokuheiji to him. Now his words in turn had sparked a fire in the magistrate. Chūnai could only marvel, and hope.

Hashimoto proved as good as his word. He went to Sendai and spoke first with his immediate superior, County Magistrate Imaizumi Shichisaburō, then set his sights on the man in charge of Sendai finances, Comptroller Kayaba Moku—an unprecedented move that should probably be called foolhardy.

Sendai magistrates in charge of political and economic affairs were the top officials; the comptroller, with authority over the budget, was below them in the chain of command. In fact, however, real power lay with Kayaba. That's because in Sendai there was something called the "three-ryō rule." The comptroller was able to reward retainers at his own discretion, in an amount not to exceed three ryō. The magistrates, in contrast, couldn't disburse any money without the daimyo's permission. Moreover, Kayaba's office was right beside the daimyo's official chamber. As comptroller, he was in charge of financial affairs, could hand out rewards, and was involved in political affairs as well. His power was vast.

Hashimoto was well acquainted with Kayaba Moku, who like him was involved in Sendai finances, although they occupied vastly different positions. Kayaba was the cynosure of all eyes, Hashimoto a petty official from the hinterland. Kayaba was touted as "the ablest official in a hundred years"—meaning the ablest official since a man named Tokita Suruga, financial wizard and right-hand man of Tadamune (1600–1658), the second lord of the house of Date.

Tokita Suruga had been a man of stubbornness and daring. One time Tadamune ordered him to pass on the secrets of finance to his juniors, but Tokita did nothing. When prodded, he replied, "Very well. There is one secret, and one only. I'd like your lordship to come hear it, too." When Tadamune gathered his chief retainers together, Tokita announced, "Here is the secret to managing domain finances: whatever you do, don't give in to the daimyo's arbitrary whims." The daimyo's vast income meant that as long as he didn't live extravagantly, he need never want for money, but if the comptroller gave in blindly to his every wish, then no amount of money would be enough, no matter what economies were practiced. He said all this to Tadamune's face. The chief retainers went pale.

It's remarkable that in the first half of the 1600s, more than a century before our story begins, a commissioner of finance should have dared to address his lord in such bold and uncompromising terms. Tadamune, far from losing his temper, commended him. Thanks to Tokita's unshakable integrity, Sendai Domain was able to bear the shogunate's stringent demands for military service and construction projects, pay all its debts, and fill the castle storehouse with gold.

Kayaba consciously modeled himself on this venerated predecessor. "Tokita Suruga used to say…" He repeated this phrase continually, thereby putting himself in the other man's league. Despite his praise of Tokita, he conducted himself in exactly the opposite way: instead of speaking hard truths to the daimyo and cutting waste, he oppressed the people. The worst came after the daimyo made an ill-advised marriage.

To establish a marriage alliance with the Tokugawa family, the shogun's adopted daughter had been chosen as a bride for Date Munemura (1718–1756), sixth head of the house of Date. Such a marriage was prestigious, an honor that satisfied the daimyo's vanity, but horribly expensive. They had had to construct a *goshuden*, the special residence a shogunal daughter was entitled to on the occasion of her marriage. All 120 shogunate guards had been engaged, plus over 100 vassal guards assigned specifically to her, for a total staff of nearly 250. The bride received an annual allowance of 6,000 ryō, an exorbitant sum that she could spend freely. The daimyo's household expenses nearly doubled, ballooning from 70,000 ryō to 130,000 ryō per year. At the same time, falling population and farmland devastation caused his annual income to shrink from 100,000 koku to 74,500 koku. One koku of rice corresponded to about one ryō. The fate of a household with an income of 74,500 ryō and expenses of 130,000 ryō was all too clear.

"Do something!" senior officials said frantically to Kayaba and his staff. The comptroller requested a land survey, but permission was denied. In Sendai Domain, high-ranking vassals given fiefs in farming villages often settled there, becoming half warrior, half farmer. A land survey would increase the tax on them as well, and so it was called off. Sendai finances went from bad to worse, and then the domain storehouse caught fire and burned to the ground. Was this the end of the house of Date? Everyone in the finance office was on edge.

But Hashimoto Gon'emon saw something he would never forget. One man only wore an unsettling, melancholy smile: Kayaba.

"Our chance has come!" cried Kayaba. After persuading his superiors, he began a campaign to expose previously untaxed "hidden paddies." Resentment swept the domain, but within the administration, the move was welcomed. Some even said it was a good thing the rice storehouse had burned down since the upshot was this new, lucrative source of income.

From then on Kayaba was untouchable. No one else had his grasp of the economy. He understood the meaning of "annual rate of return" better than most merchants. He was in a sense the first person in Sendai Domain to grasp the essence of capitalism. As he saw it, one thing decided whether a man became rich or poor: whether he charged interest or paid it. The simple logic of this principle, a basic tenet of capitalism, eluded most domain officials of that time. They borrowed money and ran domain finances into the ground. Interest was high, normally around ten percent, so having to pay interest on loans was crippling.

Kayaba stressed the crucial importance of avoiding debt. To do so, the domain had to earn money. To earn money, it had to function like a business concern and offer some product for sale. "Buy rice," Kayaba advised, so Sendai purchased rice from domain farmers and sold it at a profit in Edo, Osaka, and other cities. This rice trading system dated back to the time of founder Masamune, but under Kayaba's leadership it became organized and large-scale.

"Sendai has products but no wares," it was said. The huge northeastern domain was rich in natural resources but lacking in commodities. *Sendaihira*, a prized silk fabric used to make *hakama* trousers, didn't sell well enough to count. The one exception was rice. The large and fertile plains of Sendai produced an enormous quantity of rice, a commodity that sold well in Edo and elsewhere. Even before Kayaba's new plan was introduced, people said, "One third of the rice eaten in Edo comes from Sendai."

Kayaba made it illegal for farmers to subsist on rice they themselves grew. Harsh frugality laws were enforced. In Yoshioka, too, only samurai families ate white rice. Farmers and townsmen mixed theirs with turnips, barley, and millet. Moreover, by a clever method, Kayaba purchased rice forcibly from the farmers. Early in spring, after they had consumed all their grain and were ready to plant a new crop, he would lend them money interest-free. These loans were called *omegumikin*, "domain favor money." On the surface this policy appeared compassionate, but farmers had to pay back the springtime loan in rice at harvest time, when rice was plentiful and prices low. In this way the domain was able to buy up a huge amount of cheap grain.

Kayaba loaded the rice on boats in Ishinomaki Harbor and shipped it to Edo, where it sold at high prices, yielding a good profit margin. Rice that farmers possessed after paying their annual tribute was also bought up at low prices and sold for profit in the cities. This feature too was unique to Sendai Domain. No other domain used the staple as a means of enriching itself to this extent. Sendai effectively cornered the market on rice for export, reaping all the profit.

This rice trading system was a major factor explaining Sendai's failure to flourish despite its natural advantages. Whether domain commodities were sold by the ruling clan or by the people made a huge difference. In the Kinai region around Nara and Kyoto, where economic activities were advanced, the clans could never have operated a rice monopoly; if it had been possible to make money that way, the people themselves would have done so. In the Kinai region people grew rich, but in the far-flung regions of Tohoku and southern Kyushu, where geographical distance rendered selling commodities to Edo impractical, they did not. Instead, the domain bought up the rice and sold it. This is why in these remote areas the domain was strong, but private economic behavior remained chronically weak and undeveloped. And in times of famine, this situation could lead to tragedy.

In an age lacking modern selective breeding of plants, to grow rice, a southern plant, in the northerly Tohoku region was no easy task. On top of that, the domain had a monopoly on this staple food, without sharing any of the profit with those who grew it. Back in ancient and medieval times, Michinoku was known for its wealth from gold mining and horse breeding, but as the Edo period wore on, the population shrank and land values declined until people sang a satirical ditty about mountains up north being worth only 100 mon apiece.

In the twentieth century, Tohoku acquired a nuclear power plant and sent electricity, the staple of industry, to Tokyo. Instead of rice, they sent electricity; nothing else changed. The effects of radiation threatened to reduce the beautiful mountains of Michinoku literally to the value of one hundred mon apiece. In every age, the chosen and the wealthy have power, and they toy with the lives of the weak.

The question must be asked: Wasn't there some way for Edo-period administrators to govern Sendai for the greater benefit of its residents? Someone like Kayaba was seen as an "able administrator." If the day ever comes when an able administrator is defined as someone who takes the interests of the people to heart, that day will surely mark the beginning of the ideal state that the human race has always striven for.

Magistrate Hashimoto, however, had to confer with Kayaba. He didn't beat around the bush. "Sir, I question the judgment handed down on the Yoshioka case."

Kayaba was unaccustomed to such outspokenness, and he found it appalling. Didn't the magistrate realize that such words might jeopardize his career, or that he, Kayaba, was a man to be feared? Hashimoto had come before one of the most powerful men in Sendai government to raise an objection over a matter already settled—a clear violation of protocol; an act of madness. The man must be an idiot. But Kayaba gave no sign of his contempt; a government official must never let his personal opinions show. He decided the best course was to answer truthfully.

"That petition was no good," he said. The people involved had taken advantage of the times to seek their own selfish benefit ("selfish benefit" was one of Kayaba's pet phrases; as one who was sharply aware of where his own interests lay, he used it frequently) and so naturally their petition had been rejected. They knew full well that Lord Shigemura needed funds for the biannual procession to Edo, and therefore they'd come demanding high interest on a loan. Such an outrage was impermissible.

Hashimoto swiftly contradicted him. "That is not true, sir."

"Oh?"

"Yoshioka is under my jurisdiction, so I have looked carefully into the matter, and that simply is not the case." The Yoshioka plea was entirely legitimate and honorable, he said. It was no spur-of-the-moment way to take advantage of his lordship's problems. A man called Asanoya Jinnai had hoarded coins for years in hopes of rescuing the town from poverty, and dedicated his savings to his lordship on his deathbed. As word of his sacrifice got out, one by one others had joined the cause, pledging their own money, until there were nine in all. Asanoya's son had sold the kimono of his wife, his mother, and his children to raise more money. "So you see, sir, the truth is very different from what you had supposed." He looked Kayaba squarely in the eyes.

There was silence while Kayaba digested this. Hashimoto continued staring at him. These passing seconds would determine Yoshioka's fate.

"Oh dear," Kayaba said. The *Kokuonki* is clear on his exact words: *Yareyare.* Oh dear. Then, "Well, this is certainly an awkward state of affairs."

Hashimoto held his breath.

"In that case," said Kayaba, "I'll have a quiet word with the district headman."

That was all there was to it. Kayaba agreed on the spot to reopen the case. He sensed that unless he did, there would only be more trouble. More than that, the domain truly did need the money. The processions to and from Edo were costly, and the money from Yoshioka would be a godsend.

Though his request had been granted, Hashimoto didn't move.

"What is it?" said Kayaba. "Something else on your mind?"

"Please put in a good word with Lord Shigemura," said Hashimoto, to Kayaba's further amazement.

Hashimoto dashed home and met right away with Chūnai. "Hurry and resubmit the petition," he said, and instructed him line by line what to write. For a magistrate to reveal to a farmer the substance of government deliberations was unheard of. The domain never released information about its inner workings.

Hashimoto's willingness to do so is further indication of what a rarity he was.

"You have to write about old Jinnai," he said. "Make it clear that this project isn't something you dreamed up overnight. That might do the trick."

Chūnai was confused. "Why bring him into it?"

"If they're going to overturn their previous ruling, they have to have some pretext."

Chūnai listened.

"The point is, the nine of you didn't concoct this scheme recently. Asanoya Jinnai VI came up with the idea long ago. That has to be made clear this time around so they can grant the request. The reason for all this trouble is that it was Kayaba himself who dismissed the petition before."

Now it all made sense. Chūnai's frequent dealings with local officials gave him insight into how officials' minds worked. Probably Kayaba was planning on taking credit for granting the Yoshioka petition. Out of the goodness of his heart he had taken time to reexamine the Yoshioka case, and on encountering the moving story of a public-spirited man named Asanoya Jinnai, he had decided to grant the petition after all. This was how he intended to frame it.

What rubbish, thought Chūnai. Every town headman in the domain knew Kayaba didn't care about the plight of the farmers. The man was shameless. And yet, if this way the petition would go through, what a happy outcome that would be! Once more he wrote out the words "an offering of 5,000 kammon," the equivalent of a thousand ryō in gold. He rewrote the petition and submitted it again.

"This time our prayers will be answered," Jūzaburō thought in relief. He felt keenly the power of sincerity to move people's hearts. Magistrate Hashimoto was a man of goodwill, and even the hardhearted Kayaba had been swayed by old Jinnai's single-minded determination. A single seed contained power to make a thousand flowers bloom. Jūzaburō felt as if spring had come to the whole land.

"It's too soon to be relieved," warned Tokuheiji, but he too couldn't hide his relief. The two men waited for good news with the hope and assurance of those who wait for the spring thaw.

And yet once again their hopes turned to despair. The person responsible for their misery was again Kayaba. Here is what happened: the petition came back with a label attached. A "label" was a piece of paper attached to the bottom of a petition, containing terse instructions to either grant the petition as requested or deny it.

Edo-period government could be described as "government by label." Matters were settled largely through instructions written on glued-on labels. Ministers and other administrators kept glue and a knife at hand as they attended to government affairs. By this time in history, bureaucratic directives were no longer given orally but were always transmitted with documentary evidence—a label. The appeal of this system was that the label was a mere slip of paper, with no room to explain the whys and wherefores of the decision. This style of documentation arose simply because accountability was not sought in the government of those times. Accountability in political culture—or the lack of it—exerts a lasting impact on a country's style of government. In that sense, nothing represents Edo-period politics so well as the label system.

In any case, the petition was returned to Yoshioka. Jūzaburō and Tokuheiji gathered in an inner room of the latter's house to examine the label, and were speechless. At least the instructions were not an out-and-out rejection; that was the silver lining. But the response was devastating nonetheless: "Payment in coins being cumbersome, you will pay the thousand ryō in gold."

We're done for, Tokuheiji thought.

In their petition, they had pledged to pay the sum of 1,000 ryō in 5,000 strings of Kan'ei tsūhō coins. The impoverished townspeople had no access to gold coins known as koban, which belonged to daimyo and powerful merchants; ordinary people, unless they dealt with a money-changer, rarely if ever set eyes on them. Kayaba had spotted a loophole in this arrangement. Sendai had recently begun to mint coins, and the increased circulation had lowered their value. A thousand ryō was now valued at 5.8 million Kan'ei tsūhō. Kayaba had decided to demand the full equivalent amount, figuring that if they had to, the petitioners would somehow scrape together the rest of the money. Sensing the petitioners' desperation, he had decided to squeeze the last possible drop.

Tokuheiji had no doubt this was how Kayaba's crafty mind worked. He rued the innocent trust he had once placed in the authorities.

For the people of Yoshioka, five million coins was astronomical. Jūzaburō and Tokuheiji, along with Jinnai and the rest, had half killed themselves to cobble together their share. Now just as it seemed their efforts would be rewarded, their joy faded like a mirage. Kayaba's message was "Throw in another 800,000 coins and it's a deal." Tokuheiji bit his lip. Jūzaburō and Chisaka stared at the label, aghast. *What a dirty trick!* The unspoken words hung in the air. This response wasn't just dirty, it was disgraceful. Sendai Domain had become a grasping miser.

Their surmise was correct. Kayaba, in reviewing the resubmitted petition, had raised an eyebrow at the phrase "an offering of 5,000 kammon." Intuitively, he sensed he could get more. For Yoshioka, the petition was clearly a lifeline. If he offered to anchor that lifeline for an additional 800 kammon, how could they say no? A drowning man will grasp at a straw, but Kayaba took the concept a step further. To get a drowning man to grasp at a straw, you had to lead him to the water and make him flounder. Only he could do this, Kayaba thought.

He summoned Hashimoto and told him to have "an offering of 5,000 kammon" rewritten as "a present of 1,000 ryō in gold." The significance of the change went over Hashimoto's head. He thought Kayaba wanted to make it clear that the money was not a deposit but a gift. Little imagining that the new wording would jack up the amount by 800,000 coins, he raised no objection. "So he doesn't have the wits to see it." Kayaba smiled to himself.

An old saying has it that people with a heart aren't quick-witted, and people of quick wits have no heart.

The question was, what to do. Tokuheiji saw no way out of Kayaba's trap. "What shall we do?" he asked.

Jūzaburō had no answer. "For starters," he said, "we'll have to report this to the others."

"Yes, to Asanoya first."

The two men left Chisaka's house and headed for the Asanoya house with heavy steps.

Asanoya Jinnai had contributed 1,500 kammon, the most of any of them. He was in danger of going bankrupt as a result, and had won the sympathy of all Yoshioka. The plan itself was begun by his late father. The news would surely cause him grief. But he had to be told.

When they arrived, Jinnai came out to meet them.

"... And that's how it is," said Tokuheiji. "They're saying now that we have to give them full value for a thousand ryō, or they won't consider the petition."

"We haven't got the slightest idea what to do," said Jūzaburō.

"That's why we're here," said Tokuheiji. "To see what you think."

Jinnai listened silently as the two men spoke in turns. To their surprise, he didn't seem particularly upset. He asked one question: how much more money would be needed?

Tokuheiji explained. "The rate of exchange is 450 mon for one bu of gold, so one ryō comes to 5 kan and 800 mon. For a thousand ryō, that's 5,800 kammon. So we're short by 800 kammon."

"I see." Jinnai raised his eyes to the ceiling as if doing mental arithmetic.

Surely he didn't mean to cover the difference himself! Tokuheiji and Jūzaburō were alarmed. If he gave any more, he would be truly stone broke.

"I will provide 500 of the 800 kammon," Jinnai said. "The rest of you must somehow come up with the remainder."

Tokuheiji and Jūzaburō froze. They had to stop him from doing this, or he and his family would wind up in the street, shivering and starving. The *Kokuonki* records the expression on Sugawaraya Tokuheiji's face: "Sugawaraya wrinkled his brow." In a piece of historical writing before the advent of modern literature, it is rare to find such a realistic description of the passing expression on someone's face.

Tokuheiji could not bring himself to accept the offer. "I fully appreciate the magnitude of your offer, and the town would certainly benefit, but really, Jinnai, you mustn't do it."

Jūzaburō agreed. "If you lose everything, the rest of us will suffer. Even if we fail, why not leave our fate to heaven and try again with the original offer?"

At this the look in Jinnai's eyes darkened. For once he let loose a torrent of angry words. "No! If we don't comply, they'll never grant our request. We've climbed the mountain almost to the top—the summit is in sight. But if we do as you say, we don't have one chance in a thousand of succeeding."

He was right. Kayaba was a force to be reckoned with. If they didn't produce 1,000 ryō at current exchange rates, he would never relent. Tokuheiji knew that better than anyone. The three men were enveloped in a heavy, awkward silence. A chill came over the room, the *Kokuonki* tells us.

Just then the door slowly slid open, and Jinnai's old mother appeared. "Let me in," she said, with a glance at Tokuheiji. Everyone was startled. Women didn't come barging into men's business discussions. "From the first," she said, "the rest of the family have been prepared if necessary to sell our clothes and all we have. We've lived frugally and saved up 1,500 kammon. So…"

Tokuheiji and Jūzaburō held their breath.

"…so our minds have long been made up. All of us—me and my daughter and the grandchildren—understand that if more money is needed, all we have to do is sell our household possessions. There's no need to cause trouble for anyone else. Please let us make up the difference."

Jūzaburō wept.

Tokuheiji was overcome. There could be no greater spirit of sacrifice. He forced himself to say words that pained him to speak. "Very well. There's no help for it. Much as it distresses us, we accept your offer." He went on, "Your family has continually demonstrated its sincerity. Your offer is most touching and deeply appreciated. It is sad to have to accept it, but there is no other way."

"What a relief!" said Jinnai. "I've been prepared all along for my family to come to grief. We all realize what we're in for by taking the burden of the town on ourselves."

In this region, the verb *itamu*, "come to grief," was used to mean a family's insolvency and reduction to abject poverty. The word was properly written with characters meaning "hurt" or "damage," but people in Yoshioka used instead a character meaning "grieve" to bring out the sense of the death of a long family line. When a family was brought to grief, its members were split up and sold into servitude or slavery. In Jinnai's family, even his young grandchildren were prepared to accept this fate.

When Jinnai said, "What a relief," how cheerful he looked! When she heard him say those words, how sweetly his mother smiled! Never had either Jūzaburō or Tokuheiji seen looks of such rich contentment on any human face.

"I know of no other family so deeply united. It is a sign of true character." With these words, Jūzaburō bowed deeply and, accompanied by Tokuheiji, left the Asanoya house.

Kayaba Moku's cunning ploy meant that Jinnai and his son Shūemon ended up putting up the whopping sum of 2,000 kammon. Even then, they were short 300 kammon. Somebody would have to make up the difference. Of the nine contributors, one was holding out. His name was Hayasakaya Shinshirō.

Shinshirō's business was flourishing, and his family had become one of the richest in Yoshioka. But when it came time to pledge, he had offered a measly 300 kammon, half his rightful share. Only Zempachi, at 200 kammon, had given less. Though perfectly capable of donating 500 or 600 kammon, he had stubbornly refused to increase his pledge. Now was the time for him to step up and do the right thing, they all thought. As if he sensed which way the wind was blowing, he never came to their assemblies, no matter how they waited. Finally Tokuheiji lost patience and went to see him. Sitting knee to knee, he laid out his case while Shinshirō listened blankly.

"I can't do any more," Shinshirō said over and over. "Just leave me out of it, please."

"Nobody's saying you have to supply the entire sum. Another ninety would do."

Even then, Shinshirō balked. Finally, having run out of arguments, Tokuheiji revealed the straits that Jinnai's family was in. Only then did Shinshirō soften. With red-rimmed eyes, he said, "Let me talk it over again with my relatives and my wife."

But that was the extent of the thaw in his heart. One day, picking a time when Tokuheiji wouldn't be there, he went to Chisaka's house and said, "Even if my entire family and I went naked, we couldn't come up with even half of ninety kammon. You've got to believe me."

This was a lie. The Hayasakaya family could easily have provided forty-five kammon.

Chisaka's face grew livid. Anger rose within him, but he held his feelings in check.

Then Tokuheiji hastily joined them. One look at Chūnai's face told him what Shinshirō had said. Liar! he thought. But the next moment, something made him reconsider. He thought of the look on Jinnai's face the previous day. Before him now, Shinshirō's hands were trembling as he cowered. The man was just trying to protect his family. The fault didn't lie with him. It was the deviousness of the authorities that caused men to lie, and fall out with their neighbors, and suffer.

Tokuheiji squared his shoulders and spoke with determination. "Chisaka-sama," he said, "it seems that Shinshirō is under great stress. It was no easy thing for him to pledge the original three hundred kammon. Let's not force him."

With that, Shinshirō was off the hook. It was decided that the two men who had joined the group late, Zempachi and Shinshirō, would not have to contribute any further money, and the missing three hundred kammon would be made up equally by the other six.

They wrote out the list of contributors and the amount each had given, as in a subscription book. First came the amount of the contribution, then the name of the contributor's shop or position, his private surname (used only among friends and family), and finally his given name. Chūnai, of course, wrote his actual surname.

2,000 kammon	Asanoya	(Endo) Jinnai
550 kammon	Kokudaya	(Takahira) Jūzaburō
550 kammon	Sugawaraya	(Sugawara) Tokuheiji
550 kammon	District headman	Chisaka Chūnai
550 kammon	Town headman	(Endō) Ikuemon
550 kammon	Kokudaya	(Takahira) Jūbei
550 kammon		(Endō) Junai
300 kammon	Hayasakaya	(Hayasaka) Shinshirō
200 kammon	Kokudaya	(Takahira) Zempachi
Total 5,800 kammon	Equivalent to 1,000 ryō	

The nine men had amassed an incredible number of coins. Five thousand eight hundred kammon was the same as 5.8 million Kan'ei tsūhō. The contribution of the Asanoya Endō family was awe-inspiring. Their 2,000 kammon stood out above all the rest. The contributions of district headman Chisaka and town headman Ikuemon paled in comparison, not to mention that of Shinshirō. People in town were beginning to grumble, "With their means, they could have given more." Jūzaburō and the others understood this human tendency and worried about it—but at any rate, now the money Kayaba had demanded was in hand, all one thousand ryō.

The time finally came. It was three in the morning on July 1, 1772, when a strange sound rang out in the pitch dark. It was the sound of someone beating violently on the gate of Chisaka Chūnai's house—the sound the people of Yoshioka had been waiting for.

"The petition of Yoshioka post town is granted."

At long last, the letter of command had arrived, signed by all the magistrates of Sendai Domain. When Tokuheiji heard this, he shouted, "Thank you! We have all been waiting for the coming of this day!" and ran around town as if he had sprouted wings, knocking on the door of every contributor. The news raced through town. By sunup, people were flocking to Chisaka's house, raising cheers.

Jūzaburō, Jinnai, Ikuemon…even old Junai was there, tottering on his cane.

"Won't someone read this aloud?" Chisaka held the scroll high over his head. For a man who was normally a stickler for protocol, this was an unusually gallant gesture. Ikuemon was usually the one to read aloud any public notices. Chisaka deliberately broke precedent. All eyes turned to one man—Jinnai.

"Go on, Jinnai, you read it," someone said, and the scroll containing the letter of command was handed to him.

Jinnai took the scroll, and he too raised it high above his head in reverence. "Very well, then I will do the honors." He and his family had waited all their lives for this moment.

His voice rang out. The contents were all that they had hoped for. Their determination had finally won over the authorities. Six long years had passed since Jūzaburō and Tokuheiji had first met over tea and begun laying their plans.

Their petition was granted, but another mountain loomed. Now they had to present the money to the Sendai warehouse overseer—but they didn't yet have the full value of the thousand ryō, as Kayaba required. Now they needed to hold Miuraya Sōemon in Ishinomaki to his promise. If he refused to lend them the money, it was all over.

Was he a man of his word? It all came down to that. If, when they went to borrow the money, he went back on his word, Jūzaburō and Tokuheiji were prepared to slit their bellies and die, then and there. They took with them daggers, the requisite white kimono, and their wills. Chisaka was supposed to join them but, perhaps afraid of dying, he stayed at home, pleading illness. Ikuemon accompanied them instead. Chisaka swore that he was prepared to slit his belly in his sickbed if need be, but who knows what his real intent may have been.

It should surprise no one that a pair of farmers were readier to commit ritual suicide than an official much closer to samurai rank. Farmers and merchants of this era were like that. The sense of honor had spread throughout the land even among commoners; samurai had no monopoly on do-or-die heroics. Failure to keep their sworn promise to the authorities would have impelled Jūzaburō and Tokuheiji to choose to end their lives. Their sense of honor was simple and unschooled. The modern nation-state that came about after the Meiji Restoration made full use of this deeply instilled sense of honor to win the Sino-Japanese and Russo-Japanese wars, going on to fight in the Pacific War and ultimately suffer defeat.

But to return to our story, Miuraya did keep his word, readily agreeing to give them the promised sum of 562 ryō and 2 bu. With disarming ease, he handed it over. When Jūzaburō and Tokuheiji realized their lives had been spared, they exchanged looks, let out their breath, and laughed, feeling as if they had returned from the dead.

Finally they had acquired all the money they needed. But in the meantime, the value of low-denomination coins had continued to slide, so Jūzaburō was forced to prevail upon his son Otoemon in Sendai to supply an additional 125 ryō. Despite this additional setback, they did furnish 1,000 ryō, based on the current exchange rate, as promised. Tokuheiji went to Sendai and delivered the money to Daimonjiya, the warehouse overseer of Sendai Domain. And then he came home.

Everything was now finished. At the end of the year, as stipulated in the letter of command, an interest payment was to arrive from the domain. They could hardly wait.

But the last day of the year came and went without any word from the domain. The New Year, 1773, dawned. By February there was still no word.

"Strange." The petitioners became worried.

This must be clearly stated: after extorting money from the Yoshioka petitioners, the domain made no attempt to keep its sworn promise to pay the interest due. Instead, the nine were put in the unheard-of position of having to dun the daimyo.

First to speak up was Jinnai. On February 20 he called at Chisaka's house with Tokuheiji. "We've endured hardship for going on eight years now," he said. "We don't want any hanky-panky at the end." Of all Japan's farmers, probably he is the only one ever to have accused his lord, the daimyo, of hanky-panky.

Chisaka wasn't ready to go so far. "I can't stop worrying, either," he said. "But it's not our place to make accusations about what the government does or doesn't do." These were the words of someone looking to protect himself. However, Chisaka's connections gave him an insider's knowledge of government affairs. He went on, "Magistrate Yashima tells me that the thousand ryō we donated is still sitting in the treasury and hasn't been given to the overseer yet."

This was surprising. Despite its lack of resources, Sendai Domain was letting the thousand-ryō donation lie instead of applying it to operating funds.

By the late Edo period, government was organized hierarchically with no lateral communication.

"But the magistrate also said that it would be a good idea to make some inquiries. I was just going to do so today."

Well, Tokuheiji thought in a fury, you're certainly taking your time! The district headman didn't seem the least troubled. But the others had gone into debt to lodge this petition. They needed to obtain the interest as quickly as possible and begin paying back what they owed. The need for action was urgent.

Jinnai and Tokuheiji implored Chisaka to write a letter of inquiry to the government. A reply wasn't long in coming: "The interest will be paid. However, as the thousand ryō was received only last September, payment will begin next year."

This was a pitiful excuse, hardly befitting a domain with an income of 620,000 koku. Nor did the letter give any concrete indication of when or how payment would be made. Unsatisfied, they wrote back seeking answers, and the reply came on April 5: "Funds will be withdrawn from the finance office. Have the recipients report to Sendai." And so the domain finally agreed to make the payment. Their attitude was shabby to say the least.

On April 10, a man named Shōemon, the official transporter of cash for Sendai Domain, brought 42 ryō and 912 Kan'ei tsūhō to Yoshioka. It had been a very long time in coming.

But this isn't the end of the story. Kayaba Moku made another move.

When told the first interest payment had been made, he couldn't help feeling surprised. He knew better than anyone that he had put a series of obstacles in the nine petitioners' way, yet they had paid the thousand ryō in full. Then when the domain dragged its feet on paying the interest, they had patiently negotiated and won the day. Those farmers put samurai to shame, he thought. Among his own men, there wasn't one of the caliber of Kokudaya Jūzaburō or Sugawaraya Tokuheiji. Hashimoto had explained everything in detail: how when Kayaba ordered the thousand ryō to be paid in gold, Asanoya Jinnai and his son Shūemon had unhesitatingly increased their load of debt, taking the town's burden as their own.

"The family is all but certain to become destitute and broken. Everyone in Yoshioka feels pity for the heir." Hashimoto had wanted to add this, but bit the words back.

Kayaba was curious about the Yoshioka petitioners, particularly Jinnai, whom he strongly wished to meet. More than curiosity, he felt respect and goodwill toward him. He issued an order: "Summon the Yoshioka nine. I will receive them at my home."

This announcement caused a flurry in Yoshioka. Kayaba Moku, the powerbroker in charge of Sendai's financial and civil administration, wanted to meet them in person. They were told to present themselves on May 9 at eight in the morning. The nine men looked at each other. This was a direct order; they had no choice but to comply.

And so they set out for Sendai in a body—though Shūemon went in his father's place.

When they arrived at Kayaba's residence, the comptroller was there waiting for them. He looked around at the group and welcomed them. To their amazement, in his remarks he mentioned old Jinnai by name. "Your persistence in applying yourselves over a number of years, beginning with the generation of Asanoya Jinnai VI, grandfather of Endō Shūemon, is commendable." He then distributed award money among them.

Kayaba stared at Shūemon, wishing he could have met the father and talked to him. Something in him was drawn to the man. After the nine had left, he asked one of his men where Jinnai was.

"He stayed home because his legs hurt."

"He could have ridden here."

"Begging your pardon, sir, that could never happen."

"Why not?"

"He took an oath never to ride on horseback or in a palanquin."

Intrigued, Kayaba asked, "Why won't he ride horseback?"

"That's because of…something his late father taught him."

"Tell me."

"It seems that once some people from Yoshioka set out for Ishinomaki. Jinnai was supposed to go with them, but his eyes and legs were giving him trouble. They urged him to ride, and he told them, 'My late father taught me better. There is a book called *Myōgakun* that contains a powerful message.' Then he quoted this passage:

> Know this. Among all living creatures, human beings are primates. Therefore, for humans to cause suffering to oxen and horses by riding on their backs is cruel and should seldom be done, and to cause suffering to fellow humans by being borne on their shoulders must never be done. If you are seriously ill and carried on a stretcher, it may be forgivable, but as long as you are capable of walking or riding on a horse, you must absolutely never ride in a palanquin and so cause pain to others. Never forget that, as long as you live."

Kayaba was stunned. No teaching had ever exposed the essential contradictions of the age quite so candidly. The backbone of this doctrine was the principle that every human life is precious and no human being must ever cause suffering to another. At the same time, Kayaba perceived that the same principle would, if turned on its head, lead to a dangerous conclusion: that for one man to ride in a palanquin on the shoulders of others was an insult to the bearers' humanity. It would follow that those who rode in palanquins were thoughtlessly inhuman. Who rode in palanquins? Samurai; Kayaba and his peers, the most exalted class of people in Edo society; the daimyo, Lord Shigemura; the shogun himself. Yoshioka was mired in poverty because samurai laid the burden of forced labor on the shoulders of the townsfolk.

Kayaba shivered at this doctrine nurtured by the Asanoya family in a mountain village where cold winds blew. He was swept by a sense of emptiness.

No one knows how the mysterious book called *Myōgakun* came to be so treasured by the merchant family of Asanoya (later Endō) in Michinoku. The book evidently had incredible power over those who read it. Repeated readings had led Jinnai and his kin to embark on the plan to save Yoshioka.

Jūzaburō also remembered having repeatedly read and been inspired by the teachings in *Myōgakun*. The Asanoya family had been told it was by the great Neo-Confucian writer Kaibara Ekiken (1630–1714), but apparently this wasn't so. The Osaka publisher wanted to sell the book, so he said it was written by Kaibara, but actually it was the work of an unknown Confucian scholar named Seki Ichiraku (1644–1730) from the province of Bizen (present-day southeastern Okayama).

Bizen was the center of a school of learning known as "Bizen Shingaku" (Education of the Heart), influenced by Yōmeigaku, the Wang Yangming branch of Neo-Confucianism. Men like Nakae Tōju (1608–1648) and Kumazawa Banzan (1619–1691) were its representative spokesmen. However, Yōmeigaku was suppressed as a dangerous movement. That might well be another reason why *Myōgakun* was marketed as the work of the respected Kaibara Ekiken.

In any case, the book had an undoubted influence in shaping the beliefs of the small Asanoya family.

When Jūzaburō and the others opened the seals on the envelopes of money they had been awarded, they found that Shūemon had received three ryō and three bu, the others two ryō and two bu apiece. They returned to Yoshioka quietly in the middle of the night to avoid a scene—but it was no use. A line of people several miles long was waiting to greet them, each person with a paper lantern in hand. The *Kokuonki* records that the sight was "as beautiful to them as stars in the sky."

When they arrived in Yoshioka, someone suggested distributing the award money among everyone in town, and all agreed. At Jinnai's suggestion, they gave two hundred mon to everyone, down even to the poorest of the poor.

Starting in 1774, at the end of every year Yoshioka received interest on the thousand ryō amounting to exactly one hundred ryō. The town prospered, and its population held steady for the next century, to the end of the Edo period.

Every summer at the Star Festival, gorgeous decorations were hung on the gates of each house and shouts of joy echoed in the streets. At long last, Jūzaburō, Tokuheiji, and Jinnai had achieved their desire.

One more thing must be told. Life did not become easier overnight, or within even the first few years. Jūzaburō and the rest were afflicted by the hardships those around them had feared. Jinnai and his son, having spent such a huge amount of money, had great difficulty managing their shop. But Hayasakaya Shinshirō, who had held out on the others and contributed only a small amount of money, prospered more and more.

"The Asanoya family is going to go bankrupt," townsfolk murmured, frowning. "They say the descendants of families that accumulate good deeds reap rewards, but not always. Hardhearted families are the ones that grow wealthy."

But then Jinnai did something extraordinary. Besides the sake brewery, he ran a pawnshop that also supported the family, and now he began lending money even to the destitute, people who normally would be turned away at the door. These were people who, having lost their land to debt, were forced by hunger and cold to pawn their very clothes. Since they owned nothing of any value and had no hope of paying off a loan, any pawnbroker who did business with them faced problems. But Jinnai dealt kindly with the impoverished people who came to his pawnshop, and he kept on lending them money. Word spread, and poor people flocked to his store. Jinnai and his son Shūemon listened to them all, and sometimes refrained from taking their belongings, extending interest-free loans instead. They also forgave loans by the dozen.

Had Jinnai lost his mind? The man seemed bent on running his business into the ground. Jūzaburō and others fretted, but Jinnai appeared unconcerned. "Money exists to help people live," he said. "We have to help each other in time of need." Yet strangely enough, once he adopted this unselfish practice, his fortunes turned. If you were going to pawn something, people said, Asanoya's pawnshop was the place to go. His generosity attracted even better-off clients, and instead of collapsing, his business began to recover.

Then word that Asanoya Jinnai had come to the aid of dozens of destitute people reached the ears of domain officials. One of them told the daimyo, Date Shigemura.

Lord Shigemura, an enlightened ruler, composed *waka* poetry and was a master calligrapher. A few years back when Sendai prisons were emptied of prisoners, he had clapped his hands in jubilation and distributed food and drink to town officials.

"I'd like to meet this fellow Jinnai," Lord Shigemura said. Kayaba had once summoned Jinnai with no success, but the daimyo was determined. One day while on a tour of his domain, he stopped by Jinnai's house and invited himself in. Somewhere he had learned that the man was an accomplished calligrapher, and no sooner was he settled in the seat of honor than he said, "I understand that you are a calligrapher. Write something for me."

Jinnai was dumbfounded. But there was no ignoring a direct order from the ruler of the domain. He took up his brush, wrote something, and presented it for inspection.

Shigemura exclaimed with pleasure. Then he said, "Now it's my turn." He picked up the brush and wrote out three lines:

Frosty Night
Cold Moon
Spring Wind

"You brew sake, do you not?" he said. "Make these the names of your brands." And with that, he took his leave.

"Lord Shigemura himself christened Asanoya's sake!" The news spread like wildfire, and sake sales soared. And so in the end Jinnai was spared bankruptcy. He went on to use his personal funds for bridge and road repair.

Jūzaburō, meanwhile, continued to devote himself to business alongside his son and grandson. The yearly disbursement of interest to the town gave him his greatest joy, but he was only to witness it four times. On March 27, 1777, the fourth year since their great dream came true, he died at the age of fifty-eight. The cause of death is not known, but his last words were recorded. He made three admonitions to his children and grandchildren:

> First, never talk to other people about what I did. Never think that our family has done some good deed. Never act proudly or haughtily. Live quiet lives.
> Second, continue from now on to do all you can for Yoshioka. Remember that you can carry on your business thanks to the cooperation of others. Show your respect and appreciation.
> Third, sell tea.

The instruction to sell tea no doubt meant that they should support the business Tokuheiji had begun in order to bring prosperity to Yoshioka. As admonished, Jūzaburō's descendants stayed mum about his achievements. Privately, however, they owned a charming wooden statue of him which they revered, calling it "O-Dokko-sama." Whenever a young child in the family did something naughty, he would be hauled in front of the statue and told,

"O-Dokko-sama is watching you!" Perhaps as a result, each generation ran the family business soberly and honestly, as Jūzaburō would have wished. Other shops in town went under, but Kokudaya remains in business to this day.

Tokuheiji outlived Jūzaburō for a while. Even after the interest payments began to arrive, he continued to negotiate with the domain. "If the land tax Yoshioka pays in the fall were made equal to the interest due, that would save us the trouble and expense of going to the capital to collect the interest, and the payment could be delivered here before the New Year. Why not do that?" He badgered the domain until finally they approved the suggestion.

After the death of his beloved wife, Natsu, Tokuheiji's health failed visibly, and a year later he was gone. He was sixty-five years old. They must not have had any children, for no one took over his store, and friends organized his funeral. Since he had opened the way for the salvation of Yoshioka, they extolled him, and he received a posthumous Buddhist name with the title "Koji" (lay follower of Buddha), an honor normally reserved for high-ranking samurai. In full the name was Tokuō Dōki Koji; the first part meant literally "virtuous old man, resplendent path." They had this name carved on his grave. Since in his lifetime Tokuheiji had triumphed over samurai by virtue of his wits, the name seemed only appropriate.

The longest-lived of the nine was Jūzaburō's younger brother, Jinnai. After distributing rice and grain to starving farmers in neighboring counties during the Temmei Famine of 1784, in September 1802 he fell ill. As he lay on his deathbed, a priest from the family temple was summoned. Jinnai had donated more votive offerings than anyone, and he had served as representative of temple supporters. The grateful priest came prepared to bestow the posthumous name Zen'yo-in Jikei Koji, written with characters meaning "goodness and honor, mercy and praise." Names combining the honorary suffix "-in" with "Koji" were reserved for men of highest social standing. Asanoya had been granted permission to use the surname Endō, and since in his lifetime he had been honored with a visit from Date Shigemura, it was only natural that the temple should have bestowed on him such an august name. Besides, Tokuheiji having already been buried under a name ending in "Koji," it would not have seemed right unless Jinnai, who was from a much more illustrious family, received this still greater honor.

As his time drew near, Jinnai summoned his last bit of strength and tried to speak. A relative put an ear to his parched lips and heard him say in evident pain, "I have one wish."

"What is it?"

"I don't want a posthumous name ending with 'Koji.' Let mine end in 'Shinji,' the same as everyone else's." He said this in a weak, barely audible voice, and quietly died. He was seventy-five years old. His face was absolutely peaceful, they say.

"What humility!" The story goes that the priest muttered this on his way home, shaking his head.

And so the posthumous name carved on Jinnai's gravestone was one character shorter than planned: Zen'yo Jikei Shinji.

Translator's note: The amount raised by the Yoshioka nine is roughly equivalent in today's currency to three million U.S. dollars.

2. Nakane Tōri

(1694–1765)

Nakane Tōri (1694–1765) lived and died as a "village Confucian," and few people know about him now, but I feel compelled to write about him.

Nakane never wanted his life to be widely known. Undoubtedly he would not be pleased at my writing this essay about him. He himself made every effort to erase all trace of his existence. Therefore, historical materials are scarce, and I don't know to what extent I may be able to uncover the story of his life.

Nakane was a poet of transcendent ability. If he had followed any ordinary path, we would surely remember him as one of the greatest Japanese poets of all time. "In poetry, Nakane has no peer": this was the consensus of Edo literati in the Kyōhō era (1716–36). In the later Kansei era (1789–1801), Confucian men of letters like Shibano Ritsuzan (1736–1807), Inoue Shimei (1730–1819), and Ōta Kinjō (1765–1825) looked at the few surviving manuscripts of his poems and were astonished, declaring him "the rarest poetic genius since Keigen" (a quarter-century stretch of time covering Keichō, the last pre-Edo era, and Genna, the first era of the Edo Period). In other words, they were calling him the finest poet since the dawn of the age of Tokugawa. Throughout the Edo period, no poet before or after Nakane Tōri came close to him.

There is a reason why a poet of such outstanding ability remains unknown. He himself took everything he had ever written and threw it into the fire.

The birth of this prodigy was pure happenstance. He was born in the town of Shimoda on the coast of Izu Peninsula, a place where things of every description wash ashore. A portable festival shrine from Tosa Province, a Buddhist statue—such finds are common in this harbor town jutting out into the Pacific Ocean.

Human beings wash up, too. During the Empō era (1673–1681), an eccentric-looking young man drifted into town. He looked like a samurai, but he was evidently a vagabond. No one knew where he came from. He claimed to be from the province of Mikawa (present-day Aichi Prefecture), but there was no telling the truth of this. Drawn to nature and artistic pursuits, he would gaze at the rugged cliffs, sighing with pleasure and murmuring his appreciation for the seacoast and the small islands. He was so fond of the rocky coastline that he styled himself Takehama (rough shore) and settled in Shimoda. Also, wherever he may have acquired the knowledge, he opened a medical practice. In time he took a wife. This man was Nakane Shigekatsu, Tōri's father. In short, a samurai's aimless wanderings led him to a place of scenic beauty where he fathered a son—our mysterious poet.

Tōri's childhood name was Magohei. Little is known of his childhood, which doesn't seem to have been very happy. Though his father Shigekatsu had a flourishing practice, as the old wanderlust returned he took to drink and would stay out late until his son came after him. Clutching a lantern in his small hand, the boy would roam the streets of Shimoda looking for his drunkard father. The sight of him out on such an errand in the dark of night moved the townspeople to pity.

The following episode has been handed down. One summer night when his father was late, Tōri went out and hunted for him. Eventually he saw a figure come staggering toward him. It was his father, so blind drunk that he swore at his son, collapsed under a roadside tree, and began to snore. Striped mosquitoes swarmed around him. Tōri bravely tried to pick his father up and carry him home piggy-back, but his strength wasn't equal to the task. He had no choice but to return home alone. As soon as he opened the door, he told his mother, "Father will be staying at a friend's house tonight. There aren't enough mosquito nets, so he told me to bring one back. I'll sleep there, too." This was Tōri's first lie, told out of concern for his mother's feelings. With the mosquito net in hand, he raced back and put it up over his passed-out father. He stayed awake all night long at his father's side, or so the story goes. Of course Tōri himself never breathed a word of this incident, and his mother didn't learn about it until years later, through rumors in town.

The child's seriousness made his elders all the more anxious over his future. His mother decided he wasn't suited for the hustle and bustle of this world and would be better off as a priest. She sent him to a Zen temple, where he shaved his head and took the name Shōen.

Once he became an acolyte, Tōri took an interest in something unusual. He decided he wanted to learn Chinese: "Every morning we chant a sutra pronouncing the characters in Japanese, but Zen comes from China. I want to read the sutras in their original pronunciation." Whether he got the notion from gazing out at the far-off sea or whether it was something in his blood, an inheritance from his drifter father, is impossible to say. In any case, at the beginning of the eighteenth century, a Zen acolyte in rural Japan took this uncommon idea into his head.

At the time there were only two places in Japan where the Chinese language was readily acquired. One was the Chinese residential district in Nagasaki, the other Ōbakusan Mampukuji Temple in Uji. Tōri chose the latter.

Ōbakusan Mampukuji was a small Chinese cosmos. Ingen (1592–1673; Yin Yuan in Chinese), the founder of the Ōbaku school of Zen Buddhism, came to Japan in 1654, just around the fall of the Ming dynasty, probably to escape the disaster of having his home country overrun by foreigners. He loaded all things Chinese into a boat—an ark, so to speak—and brought them with him to the eastern archipelago. The boat contained some thirty Chinese monks as well as carpenters and plasterers. In addition, there were cooks, dining tables, and edible plants including kidney beans—to this day known as *ingen-mame* in Japanese. Ingen tried to recreate his home country on Japanese soil, planting a garden and even uprooting local bamboo to plant a grove of giant Chinese bamboo (*Phyllostachys pubescens*). He created a miniature China within Japan, a place where the Chinese language was spoken.

In the autumn of 1711, Tōri left his temple and headed for Uji. To get there he sailed to Osaka and traveled overland, staying along the way at Henjōin Temple in Nakayama, Settsu Province, where the monks invited him along on a mushroom-hunting expedition. They feasted that night on a rich haul. Tōri had never tasted anything so delicious in his life. But the next day, four of the six monks began to thrash around with a high fever. The skin on their backs festered and turned purple, and one after another they died. The youngest victim, Roshin, was eleven.

Tōri arrived grief-stricken at Ōbakusan.

There is a certain protocol at Zen temples. The aspiring novice shouts out, "*Tanomimashō*" (I ask your favor), and the head of the temple comes out and says "*Do-re*" (Let's see). He then rejects the applicant with this line: "This temple is full, and we have no nourishment to offer you, either. You are forbidden to apply for admission." This is only a means of forcing the applicant to remain at the entrance for three days, kneeling with his forehead on the ground, after which he will be admitted without fail. Everything in the world of Zen Buddhism is formalized in this way.

At Ōbakusan, studying under Chinese monks, Tōri made rapid strides in Chinese. Life there was enjoyable at first, but after a while he became dissatisfied. For someone of his curiosity, life in a Zen temple was bound to be monotonous. The temple library contained a mountain of, classics brought over from China that he was eager to read, but the monks were dismissive: "Zen training has nothing to do with books." With that, Tōri's interest in the Ōbaku school of Zen Buddhism faded. To say the spirit of Zen resides in daily routine was all very well, but any school that frowned on the reading of books was not for him.

Someone then told Tōri about a man in Edo named Sorai. "He's learned and attracts followers with his writings. He's engaged in a new kind of scholarship. As for Chinese, he prides himself that no one knows the language better than him. Aren't you from Sagami Province? That's not far from Edo. Why don't you go study with him?" The man referred to was Ogyū Sorai (1666–1728), the great Confucian philosopher of that era.

Once he saw what to do, Tōri was quick to act. He took off for Edo and never stopped on the way. His objective was the large Pure Land temple Renkōji in Komagome, founded by Toda Ujisada (1657–1733), the lord of Ōgaki Domain in Mino Province. The chief priest, a man of literary talent named Egan, was one of Sorai's followers. (From the Meiji era on, books referring to Tōri give this monk's name as Yūyo Reigan, but by this year Reigan was already dead; it seems likely that Egan's name was transmitted erroneously.) Tōri hoped a connection with Egan would provide an opening for him to become acquainted with Sorai.

For Tōri, becoming a Zen monk had never been a good idea. In order to read books while in holy orders, he was far better off with a laxer sect such as the Pure Land school, the sect that imposed fewest restrictions. To be sure, some misguided Pure Land priests led dissipated lives, running profitable houses of gambling or spending money on prostitutes, but many others, like Egan, were erudite and drawn to literature.

"Oho, so you studied Chinese at Ōbakusan, did you?" Egan leaned forward with eager interest.

A slight digression.

China held a fascination for Edo-period literati of an intensity that we today can scarcely comprehend. In gardens, calligraphy, and painting, continental taste was revered, but Japan was a closed country and foreign travel was strictly forbidden. As a substitute for going to China in person, people wanted to at least have a Chinese stone or two for their gardens, and many were imported. Taihu stone, a kind of limestone produced on the shores of Lake Taihu, was especially prized. Someone of the rank of village headman generally had one of these stones either in his garden or in a pot to gaze on with pleasure. Anyone literate in Chinese couldn't have helped being interested in a person who could actually speak the language.

Egan studied Tōri's face as if he were a rare and valuable bit of flotsam from the continent. "Won't you stay in our temple for a while?" he said.

During his stay, Tōri's behavior was peculiar. He huddled in a private room piled high with sutras and read from morning to night; it's not even clear that he took regular meals. At intervals he would let out a whoop of delight, to others' consternation. A rumor started that at nineteen, he was planning to read the entire set of scriptures—over five thousand in all. An old saying has it that many want to enter the Buddhist priesthood, but few try to read the vast sutra collection in its entirety. The monk Saichō (767–822), founder of Enryakuji on Mount Hiei in Kyoto, is said to have pulled off that monumental achievement at the age of nineteen. Yet Tōri didn't seem out to compete with Saichō. Rather, as someone in training to be a priest, he couldn't rest until he had read every sutra in existence.

Egan, the chief priest, found Tōri's diligence pleasing. The young scholar already showed considerable breadth of learning, and the retentiveness of his memory was remarkable. If, as he was reading, he came upon an expression he couldn't understand, he would keep it in mind for a matter of years, or as long as necessary until something came along to clear it up. Egan delighted in showing Tōri off to visitors. "He devotes years to the reading of a book! This is no ordinary man."

Eventually, word of the prodigy reached Sorai, who came to Egan and begged "the pleasure of being allowed to meet him"—language needlessly polite, coming from a scholar of his stature.

A brief explanation of Sorai's significance in the history of ideas is in order. The world of Confucian studies in Edo was then in turmoil, and the chief cause was Sorai, who claimed, "Confucianism today is twisted out of shape. I alone teach true Confucianism." This radical approach attracted followers. In Sorai's view, Confucianism had been distorted by the Song dynasty scholar Zhu Xi (1130–1200), whose Neo-Confucian school was in error. Present-day Confucianism was based on the teachings of that pseudo-scholar, not Confucius himself. This assertion was a fine way to start a fight, and as a means of attracting students it came with the perfect guarantee—a promise that if you studied with him you would learn the real thing. Indeed, people called incessantly at his school.

Sorai was a scholar of a decidedly political stripe. In temperament he was less like a scholar than a broker skilled at forming factions. His temperament was shaped by his upbringing. His father had been the attending physician to Tokugawa Tsunayoshi (1646–1709), later the fifth shogun, but somehow he fell out of favor and was exiled to Mobara in Kazusa (present-day Chiba Prefecture). From the age of fourteen, Sorai suffered hardship as the son of a *rōnin*, or masterless samurai. He turned to scholarship to get on in the world. Clutching his few books in that remote outpost, he pushed himself. He developed a warped ambition, and when he returned to Edo at the age of twenty-five he opened a school across from the temple Zōjōji, the family temple of the Tokugawa, in the hope of developing connections with high government officials. Sorai understood that striking up friendships with the temple priests would help him achieve distinction. And indeed, just as planned, he became the *jushin*—Confucian scholar and vassal—of Yanagisawa Yoshiyasu (1658–1714), the powerful shogunal advisor. No ordinary Confucian could match his political acumen. His skills were innate.

But Sorai had one failing. His scholarship contained an element of bluff. Since he took others' commentaries as distortions, it was incumbent on him to present true Confucian teachings. To that end, borrowing a concept from Ming China, he said it was necessary to study ancient rhetoric—the style of China's ancient classics. The only way to understand the true teachings of Confucius, he maintained, was to absorb the language of that era and become versed in ancient rhetoric. Sorai let on that he was a master of Chinese when actually he didn't know the language all that well. He merely drew on the expertise of Okajima Kanzan, a former Chinese interpreter in Nagasaki, to establish himself as an authority.

At this time Sorai was making strenuous efforts to expand his school. He called on feudal lords and visited temples, turning to all sorts of places to find people with any interest in learning and inviting them to join. He was particularly on the lookout for promising youths. He sought out buried talent, made such people his followers, and so shored up his support. When he heard about Tōri—a youth of twenty who knew Chinese and had read the Buddhist canon—he must have perked up.

At his first meeting with Tōri, Sorai commented approvingly on the young talent's studiousness, but he was not about to be outshone. Assuming an air of importance, he said, "You say you can read Chinese poetry. Try this." He handed him a volume—Li Panlong's (1514–1570) *White-Snow Tower Collection.*

"Yes, sir." Tōri took the book and began to read aloud effortlessly, to Sorai's consternation.

Li Panlong was a Ming scholar of the Late Revival School who had called for a revival of classical modes of High Tang poetry; Sorai's theories were based largely on his thinking. His poetry was written in an archaic style that no young man of twenty or so could be expected to sight-read. "That's enough," said Sorai. "Return it to me tomorrow, marked for reading in Japanese." The reason for this request was simple: he would use the prodigy to assist him in his translation of Li Panlong's works. Sorai was calculating. He made people do things to his own advantage, although he never let this motive show on the surface.

Tōri did his best to meet Sorai's expectations. He stayed up all night inscribing the book with guide marks to allow it to be read in Japanese, and quickly returned it. The master lavished praise on this feat and granted Tōri permission to become his pupil.

Tōri was elated. He felt inspired to write poems of his own in classical Chinese. For Japanese people, writing poetry in Chinese is anything but easy. The rules of meter and rhyme must be followed. Poets used to manage the task by importing special dictionaries of rhyme and meter which they relied on heavily as they composed. Partly for that reason, Chinese poetry by Japanese poets is typically stiff. Chinese who came to Nagasaki would take one look at their work and hold their noses, complaining "They smell Japanese!"

Tōri was different. He was at home in Chinese, like a winged horse in the sky. His thoughts fell naturally into poetic lines, and in short order he had written a dozen poems.

Sorai's response was surprisingly cold. He leafed through half of them and didn't bother to read the rest. Such poetic genius was of no use to him. All he wanted was a faithful follower who could help with the school of ancient rhetoric he envisioned. As he flipped through the booklet, he ignored the poems' excellence and instead began asking himself how he might turn Tōri's formidable gifts to his advantage. Then, looking up, he said, "Anyone who wishes to learn to write should read *The Commentary of Zuo, The Records of the Grand Historian*, and *The Book of Han*."

Obediently, day after day Tōri read the ancient *Commentary of Zuo*. He not only read it but began writing an introduction. He thoroughly digested and adapted the style of the commentary to use in his introduction, and when it was finished he went back to Sorai.

"Good!" exclaimed Sorai. "I'll add an inscription for you." He dipped his brush in ink and wrote on the last page of the booklet, "No longer the unlettered man of yore." Sorai was fond of dramatic gestures of this sort. The word for "unlettered" he used was a reference to the ancient general Lü Meng (178–220), who was mocked for his illiteracy.

Overjoyed, Tōri promptly wrote a biography of Lü Meng, naturally adopting the archaic prose style of historical writing prior to the Qin and Han dynasties. This effort Sorai praised to the skies. He turned to assembled guests in a packed room and declared, "Everyone, only when you have done this can you say you have thoroughly learned the *Commentary of Zuo*." Tōri had truly become Sorai's apostle. His name spread throughout the capital.

But as his literary star rose, Tōri's spirits fell. There was a lump in his chest that never went away, and finally he took to his bed. As he lay in his monk's cell in the temple rear, unable to sit up, he stared blankly at the ceiling. A ray of sunlight shone into the room and lit up the surface of his desk. As if seeking that light, he reached out an arm, emaciated from illness. His hand happened to land on a book, and he picked it up for no reason. As he riffled through it, he came to the chapter on Mencius's "vast, flowing nature." He read the words hungrily.

"I venture to ask the master what he means by his vast, flowing nature." The master replied, "It is difficult to describe. It is exceedingly great and exceedingly strong. Nourished by rectitude and sustaining no injury, it fills all between heaven and earth."

As he read, Tōri was electrified. He later wrote that this experience changed his life. He felt the universal life force animating all things. What had he been fretting over all this time? The respect of one's teacher, literary fame, ascetic training—all now seemed trivial and lackluster. He mustn't look down and busy himself in gathering grains of sand when if he raised his eyes he might discover an ocean of vast beauty.

"The way is broad and straight!" he exclaimed. All was clear.

Ever since entering the Zen temple, Tōri had been tormented by a certain story. An old woman provided shelter for a hermit and looked after him for twenty years. She always had a girl take him meals and wait on him. One day she told the girl to put her arms around the hermit and say invitingly, "How about some of this?" He pushed her away. "I am like a withered tree on top of a cliff, with no warmth." When she heard this, the old woman said, "For twenty years I've been sheltering such a vulgar, worthless monk?" She threw him out and burned down the hermitage.

This is a famous Zen koan, or riddle, known since ancient times as one of the most difficult of all. What to make of it? The question had been gnawing at him. Now the answer crystallized before him. In his later years, he would explain the answer to people, but no written account survives. He must have been able to shed some sort of fixation. He decided to leave holy orders and return to secular life.

But leaving was not allowed. The biggest obstacle was his mother, who wanted him to become an eminent priest. A devout woman who took pride in her son's being a member of the clergy, she had recently lost her husband of many years. Every day, she would kneel before Shigekatsu's memorial tablet, palms pressed together, and say with tears rolling down her cheeks, "Magohei has become a priest, so you can obtain birth in the Pure Land." Her words reflected the saying "If one child takes the tonsure, nine generations will be saved." To Tōri this was mere folk superstition, but to his mother it was perfectly real.

In any case, Tōri went back home. His footsteps were heavy. He told his mother he wanted to return to secular life, but she wouldn't allow it. If she had actually said the words "I won't allow it," he would have felt better. Instead, as soon as he told her what he wanted to do, she was stunned into silence and only bent over and pressed her forehead to the floor, quietly sobbing. Then he heard her say, "A child like you could never succeed as a scholar."

Not knowing what else to do, Tōri sent for his uncle, a rather educated man who knew of Tōri's reputation in Edo poetry circles. This uncle spoke up in his defense. Laying a hand on the mother's shoulder, he said, "A Buddhist priest has to abandon the world. So giving up a child to the priesthood means abandoning him. Parents seeking salvation by abandoning their own child… when you think about it that way, it's a cruel thing. Now Magohei wants to leave the priesthood. You'll be regaining a child. I join with your son in asking you to listen to him, and let him return to secular life."

At that, his weeping mother grew still. Tōri's leaving the priesthood was approved.

Egan, the chief priest of Renkōji, was a man of deep discernment. On hearing Tōri's decision, he said calmly, "Then you'd better stay here in another room until your hair grows out." He had a room prepared where Tōri could wait while his hair grew long enough to wear in a topknot. Treatment of priests who had returned to the laity was harsh in those days. It was considered blasphemous for one who had vowed to become a disciple of Buddha to go back on his vow and return to society. Those who let their hair grow at home were likely to be subjected to jeers and worse; throwing stones at the house of a renegade priest was commonplace. With that in mind, Egan offered Tōri a safe haven in the temple.

As he began the process of secularization, Tōri read more books than ever. "The days weren't long enough for him to read all he wanted to," says *The Philosophy of Japanese Yangminism*.

A stumbling block came from an unexpected quarter: Sorai, who expressed displeasure on hearing of these plans. He would have preferred Tōri to stay on as he was indefinitely, mingling with priests of various sects, studying Chinese, annotating texts, and generally supporting him, in Sorai's work. As far as he was concerned, that was Tōri's sole utility. His leaving the priesthood would mean a net loss. But Sorai cunningly kept his feelings to himself and went after Tōri by using a forced interpretation of the pupil's moral obligation to his teacher. "Why didn't he talk it over with me?" he complained. "If he intends to give up the priesthood and make his way as a scholar, shouldn't he have come first to me, his teacher, with the idea? And yet for over a hundred days now he's been letting his hair grow out! What's the meaning of this?"

At first Tōri didn't believe that Sorai was really angry. It seemed impossible that his teacher would ever say such things or be upset if he decided to return to secular life. On realizing that Sorai's anger was genuine, he was alarmed. He poured his heart and soul into a letter justifying his decision. It was a superb piece of prose, appealing to the emotions and flawlessly logical, but all it did was pour oil on the flames of Sorai's wrath.

"That little so-and-so," he told two other followers of his, Dazai Shundai and Yamagata Shūnan. "He's gone against me!" Even in the midst of his fury, he remained collected. Seeing Shundai's indignation, he told him, "Lead the rebuttal." Outrageously, Sorai himself did nothing and only prodded his other students to mistreat Tōri. They promptly banded together and started to ostracize him.

Tōri's next move is astonishing. One day he started a fire in the kitchen stove and threw in all his manuscripts. He was ashamed that even for a short time he had sought literary fame by relying on Sorai's spurious reputation. And so all that he had written—works of classical poetry and prose said to be unsurpassed since the dawn of the age of Tokugawa—went up in smoke.

But the story doesn't end there. Tōri's true life was about to begin.

Tōri was worried. Once he left the temple, he had nowhere to go.

Again, Ogyū Sorai's hidden power was brought to bear. Ever since Sorai had let his displeasure with Tōri be known, Tōri's peers had found one pretext or another to distance themselves. As a priest who had abandoned his vows, Tōri couldn't return home, nor could he impose any longer on Egan. One evening, lingering at the window in his quarters, he saw a beautiful sunset. A flock of geese flew past, orderly in their formation; he sensed that they were heading toward a definite destination—home. "Birds have nests to return to. I have no home. Nowhere under heaven is there an inch of space that would take me in." Despite himself, his eyes filled with tears.

Then a voice called, "You have a visitor." Hastily he composed himself and went out to the reception area. There sat a samurai of around sixty, his back ramrod straight, his eyes piercing. Tōri recognized him at once.

When Tōri first came to the temple, a small memorial service had been in progress. A four-year-old girl had died, and in a corner of the grounds was her grave, marked with a simple stone engraved with her posthumous name and the year. The father had been sitting straight, but beside him his young wife had been pitiably distressed. That was the first time Tōri had seen this elderly samurai. He remembered that someone from the temple had whispered "Poor Hosoi. A man of such ability, and yet he's a *rōnin*. With no stipend, he lives in dire poverty. This makes the third child they've lost."

Only then had Tōri realized that this impoverished and bereaved father was Hosoi Kōtaku (1658–1735), the most famous *rōnin* in the land and the most accomplished master of both scholarship and the martial arts. He was also a superb calligrapher in the Chinese style; Emperor Reigen coveted his works and sent for them all the way from Kyoto. Hosoi furthermore had a reputation as man of high integrity. The forty-seven *rōnin* who avenged their lord had consulted him before carrying out their plan, and he had written the note they planted in the ground at Kira's mansion detailing their motives and listing all forty-seven names. Even Tōri knew all this, cut off though he was from society. That very man was now here to see him.

Originally, Hosoi had been the vassal of Yanagisawa Yoshiyasu, that bakufu official of unrivaled power. He had had a stipend of two hundred koku and served as commander of an artillery unit. But he had ended up throwing all that away in the course of a single day.

The word *gikyō*, "chivalry," was made for him.

Tōri knew the story. A *rōnin* acquaintance of Hosoi's had been in desperate straits and asked his friend to help him find government work. Hosoi decided to try. His friend owned a famous sword known as the "Lion King," and when Hosoi introduced him to the chief retainer of Chamberlain Matsudaira Terusada, he was told, "If you present that sword to his lordship, I will act as middleman." Reluctantly, his friend had complied. After that he waited and waited, but no word came. Finally Hosoi consulted Terusada, who was evasive. "I don't know anything about it," he said. "That chief retainer who promised him a position is dead now. If that's what this is about, I'll return the sword."

This response clearly violated samurai honor. Hosoi was furious. "A daimyo should respect samurai. How can it be that without the slightest regard for the *rōnin*'s situation you would borrow his sword and, when you grew tired of it, return it without shame? He's been waiting for three years!" Hosoi then looked the daimyo in the eye and said in a resounding voice, "What you have done is despicable." Then he left.

Naturally that wasn't the end of it. Terusada used the foul tactic of notifying Hosoi's daimyo, Yanagisawa Yoshiyasu. Yanagisawa was also unfair, choosing to side with his fellow daimyo and casting his vassal Hosoi aside. Hosoi knew his lord's temperament and, to avoid causing any trouble, chose to resign. Ever since, he too had been a *rōnin*.

"Hosoi didn't even have enough money to move out," Tōri's informant had said that first day. "He borrowed the money from his elder brother's wife. In the meantime, Yanagisawa's vassals all grow fat on what they receive. Hosoi is a man of utter integrity. You have to feel sorry for his wife. Besides suffering poverty, they lost one daughter and then another; now this makes three. The sight of him praying at that tiny grave is so sad."

All this Tōri clearly remembered. What could Hosoi want with him?

It was Hosoi who had launched Tōri's teacher, Ogyū Sorai, on the path to success. At thirty-one, Sorai had been going nowhere in the city until Hosoi, perceiving his academic prowess, not only recommended him to Yanagisawa Yoshiyasu but provided him with a rice allowance for fifteen retainers and even found him a wife. But now that Hosoi had been ousted, far from coming to his aid, Sorai turned a blind eye. Now Sorai was sitting pretty with an income of five hundred koku, while his benefactor, Hosoi, was a lowly *rōnin* struggling with poverty and watching his small daughters die.

Actually, no one made Sorai feel more ill at ease than Hosoi. It had always been that way. At his first audience with Yoshiyasu, Hosoi had acted as intermediary and generously praised Sorai's Chinese poems. "All right then," said the daimyo, and pointed to some flowers in a nearby vase. "Write a poem on those flowers."

Sorai was put on the spot. If his effort was clumsy, he would get off to a bad start. He wished to avoid that. His sharp eyes told him that the flowers weren't real, so he responded, "Those flowers are artificial, your lordship. In ancient times, such things did not exist, so you must forgive me." With this logic—there having been no artificial flowers in the Tang dynasty, it would be inappropriate to write about them in a Chinese poem—he tried to talk his way out of the difficulty.

But such niceties were lost on Hosoi. "It's the essence of literature to write poems about things that don't exist, isn't it?" he said innocently. "His lordship has given the command. Go on, write something!"

There was no help for it. Sorai sweated and came up with a poem or rather an absurd piece of doggerel.

Even thereafter, Hosoi constantly got under Sorai's skin and made him resentful. Hosoi himself, however, was unaware of these undercurrents, and after becoming a *rōnin* he continued to freely call on Sorai. "I'm going to publish a book," he would say, and invite Sorai to do him the honor of writing the foreword. In this way, he maintained his friendship with the younger man.

Tōri seated himself gingerly before Hosoi, who at once pressed his forehead to the floor in a posture of deep humility.

"I have a most earnest request. I have heard that you are returning to secular life. Would it be possible for you to stay a while at my house? If such an arrangement would be suitable to you, of course."

Tōri was speechless. This was the height of absurdity: the greatest calligrapher in the land, a master approaching the age of sixty, prostrating himself in front of a youth barely twenty years old and asking him to lodge in his house. Tōri was grateful but mystified.

"Thank you, but I don't have a penny to my name. I couldn't possibly impose on you."

"What are you saying? Who would charge an honored guest for meals?

My house is ramshackle, but you needn't worry about paying board."

Needless to say, this was all Egan's doing. Concerned about Tōri's welfare, the chief priest had privately approached Hosoi with the proposal. Hosoi knew of Tōri's prodigious literary gifts, and he was incapable of ignoring anyone who was suffering unjustly. Hearing that Tōri was being ill-treated by Sorai's followers, he had hurried over.

The upshot was that Tōri went to stay with Hosoi at his home in Hongō. It was indeed a ramshackle place, with small children who periodically had loud crying fits. Normally, this would have been no place to bring a guest.

No sooner did they arrive than Hosoi pulled out a scroll with a long list of names. Taking up his brush, at the very end he wrote "Nakane Magohei." Seeing Tōri's look of surprise, he explained. "This is my roster of friends. Calligraphy reflects the mind, they say. The wrong friends would have a bad effect on my mind, and I wouldn't be able to write well. To remind myself to seek out proper friends, I write down their names here." This was one of his eccentricities.

Tōri was amazed by Hosoi's library. The room contained rubbings and epigraphs, not to mention Manchurian writing. Every kind of script and writing was represented; Hosoi was even familiar with Latin script. While in Nagasaki he had acquired knowledge of Western astronomical surveying and could say the names of the constellations and the months of the year in both Dutch and Latin.

"The first month of the year is Yanuwari, and the second month is Heburuwani. If you divide the world into four parts, they are Ajiya, Eroppa, Rimia (Africa), and America. If you divide it into five parts, then you count North and South America separately. One foot corresponds to one shaku, two bu by our reckoning."

When guests came, he would explain these things. Later he wrote them down in a secret book called *Confidential Letters on Surveying*. (A handwritten copy of this book survives. Philosopher Kanō Kōkichi (1865–1942), the first head of Kyoto Imperial University's Department of Literature, learned of it, and fortunately in recent years it has been reproduced. I have seen a reproduction.) In any case, Hosoi's thinking was extremely wide-ranging; Ogyū Sorai's range of thought was far narrower by comparison.

The more Tōri had to do with Hosoi, the less he knew what to make of him. His host's two daily meals, morning and night, were simple in the extreme, and he wasn't a drinker. Only when there was bonito sashimi would he indulge in a little salted sake. But he was inordinately fond of soba noodles and ate them once every three days. What puzzled Tōri most was the way Hosoi hardly slept. He read and wrote all night long. Toward dawn he would go to sleep, but when the sun came up he rose and went back to his books. He took no students, and although he produced works of calligraphy, he didn't accept money or goods for them. He didn't even appear ambitious to serve a daimyo. Only when someone brought him the noodles he loved would he weaken and hand over a piece of calligraphy in exchange. If his manservant stole rice or firewood or charcoal, he would defend him: "He wouldn't do such a thing in anyone else's house. Don't scold him."

In Tōri's eyes Hosoi was an eccentric, but his eccentricity lent his words a peculiar charm. When he spoke about topics like honor especially, he could move his listeners to tears. Why was a man of such caliber living this way? Tōri once worked up his courage to ask him.

"Sensei, you are a master of scholarship and calligraphy, the sword and the spear, archery and horsemanship, judo, firearms, and even astronomy. Why aren't you in government service? It seems such a waste."

Hosoi looked surprised. "Is that what you think? I do calligraphy because I want to, and I read books because I want to. That's enough. To me that is the way of art. If you perfect your art, the way will show itself. The modern approach is to try to make your art serve you when you reach a certain level of mastery, but I decided not to turn it into a livelihood. Make your art your path, and your path your art. I want to live by that principle." He gently smiled.

It was true. The arts were beautiful in and of themselves. It was wrong to try to use them for personal gain. In Edo when his writings won praise and he started to make a name for himself, Tōri had come close to losing his way. Glad at finding acceptance, he had kept writing poetry in a bid to win yet wider approval. Even though he hadn't been motivated by ambition, bent on a position in government service, it had still been a profanation of art.

I can't go on staying here forever, he told himself. Just as he was beginning to sense that it was time to leave the Hosoi home in Hongō, he received an unexpected invitation.

A letter arrived from the Kaga Domain residence, also in Hongō. Word had spread of a literary prodigy in the neighborhood. The letter was signed "Muro Shinsuke." Muro's pen name, by which he is commonly known, was Kyūsō. Though influential in the government of Shogun Tokugawa Yoshimune (1684–1751), he was originally a vassal of the lord of Kaga Domain (present-day Ishikawa and Toyama prefectures). "I'll soon be going to Kanazawa. Won't you accompany me?" That was the gist of the message.

At the time, Kaga Domain was on the lookout for Confucian scholars. The lord of the domain, Maeda Tsunanori (1643–1724), a formidable scholar in his own right, had a passion for collecting. Indeed, to Tsunanori scholarship was "collecting." His approach bore resemblance to the European Age of Enlightenment, which saw the creation of encyclopedias, zoos, museums, and department stores—all ways of storing and displaying large collections in a small space. Tsunanori used his income of a million koku to collect rare books and classics, and he had a keen eye for people as well. Kyūsō, one of those he "collected," had been summoned to Kaga at fifteen. Through him, the daimyo combed the world of Confucian scholars to assemble a large stable of literati. Above all, he saw Kyūsō as the most powerful opponent of Ogyū Sorai, who had driven Tōri away.

But the more time Tōri spent with Hosoi, the less he cared about Ogyū Sorai. One thing only interested him: there were books in Kaga, and he wanted to read them. "Kaga is the library of Japan": this had been the judgment of the late Confucian scholar Arai Hakuseki (1657–1725), and it was true. Unable to open a shogunal government in Kaga, the Maeda clan had instead opened a library. Books fetched high prices in Kaga, and as scholars and booksellers caught on to this, books gravitated there from far and wide. Tōri yearned to read them all.

In January 1716, twenty-two-year-old Tōri traveled with fifty-eight-year-old Kyūsō to the city of Kanazawa. In his looks, his attire, and his scholarship, Kyūsō was proper and decorous. Only his eyebrows slanted downward in a rather odd way. Unlike Sorai and Hosoi, he wasn't eloquent, but his writing was well out of the ordinary. Even his rival Sorai acknowledged the excellence of his epitaphs.

One day out of the blue Kyūsō received a call from a mischief-prone student of Sorai's named Hirano Kinka. Intending to see how good Kyūsō really was, Hirano held out a composition of his own, one he was particularly proud of, and asked him to correct it. At first Kyūsō declined, but when Hirano pressed him, he scanned the essay, crossed out twenty characters and added five, then handed it back. Miffed, Hirano then showed the corrected essay to Sorai, hoping to be told it read better without the corrections. Instead, Sorai marveled at the essay's compact perfection.

Hosoi was happy to hear that Tōri would be accompanying this learned man to Kanazawa. "You have a rare poetic gift. If that gift is burnished by Muro Kyūsō, who knows what heights you may attain?" His eyes shone.

Kyūsō was a master of neo-Confucianism, and as such he liked to have everything follow proper form. He said to Tōri, "I understand that as a priest you were called Shōen. What will you do for a name now?"

"I was intending to go back to my childhood name, Magohei."

"That's fine, but why not take a name that's a little more fitting for a samurai? I thought of one for you. What would you say to calling yourself Sadaemon? The character for 'Sada' means 'correct.' You are returning to the correct path. The Analects says 'The superior man is not merely firm but correctly firm.' Above all, there is no deviation in you. You stand straight and never bend your principles. I cannot think of a better name to express this quality than Sadaemon. That's what you should be called. Don't worry about anything in Kanazawa. All you need to do is pursue learning."

Tōri listened with a lump in his throat. "Sir, thank you for words I hardly deserve. My lifelong dream is coming true. I will fetch water for you or cook for you. Just keep me by your side." In spite of himself, he broke down and wept.

And so Tōri became Sadaemon. Kyūsō must have been happy to have him for a student, for he wrote to friends and acquaintances explaining the name he had christened him with.

Despite his promise, Tōri neither fetched water nor cooked meals. To expect him to do such things would have been unreasonable. He was a scholar first and last, of no use at such mundane tasks. Kyūsō wrote in a letter, "Every morning when he gets up, he meditates and then reads the Four Books. He's like a clay figurine." Whether meditating or reading, Tōri sat so perfectly still, impervious to mosquito bites and swarming flies, that the people of Kanazawa were amused and wondered aloud if he was made of clay. Kyūsō found this trait endearing.

Once again Tōri began a time of formidable studying, setting out to climb yet another peak of learning. After going to Mampukuji as a child and learning Chinese from Chinese monks, he had sought, like Saichō before him, to read all the Buddhist scriptures by the age of nineteen; he had studied ancient rhetoric under Ogyū Sorai and lived with Hosoi Kōtaku, who was knowledgeable in Western astronomy. To top it all, he was now pursuing orthodox Confucian studies under the most learned man of the times, Muro Kyūsō. That he was able to absorb the essence of each of these diverse branches of learning is rather miraculous.

As Tōri's fame grew in Kanazawa, word got out that he was available for hire as a Confucian scholar. "It would be a shame to have a man of such talent be taken by another domain," people said. "They should pin him down here quickly." Kyūsō shared this opinion. One reason that he had brought Tōri to Kanazawa in the first place was to see him gain employment there. He advised Tōri to take the job, but Tōri wasn't interested. "I have no desire to take a paid government position," he said flatly. "It would be inappropriate to take money for engaging in scholarship."

At first Kyūsō took this disclaimer for modesty, assuming lightly that as Tōri began mingling with people in Kanazawa his opinion was bound to change. But Tōri showed no sign of changing his mind. No matter how many times Kyūsō broached the matter, he remained adamant. As Kyūsō grew increasingly impatient, Tōri too became concerned. The longer he stayed in Kanazawa, the more pressure there would be for him to accept a job.

Finally one day Kyūsō summoned him. "You say you won't go into government service. Then what are your plans?"

"I plan to return to Edo."

"And do what?"

"Read books. I haven't read to my satisfaction yet."

"I take it that when you have done that, you'll enter government service. Very well, I'll wait."

"No, sir, I will never work for the government as long as I live."

Kyūsō was dumbfounded. "What are you saying? How can you go on reading? You can't support yourself that way."

This was true. He might have managed in a country village, but Edo was a bustling city where the cost of living was high. Even Sorai had struggled to promote his own academy in Edo. Tōri, who was stubborn by nature and lacked eloquence, had little chance of accomplishing anything similar. He would end up dying by the side of the road.

But Tōri had an answer: "I'll make *zōri* and sell them." *Zōri* were sandals woven of straw and old cloth.

Kyūsō was silent.

"I'll read day and night, and when I run out of food I'll make *zōri* and sell them. When I can afford it, I'll have a bowl of millet gruel and then go back to my books."

He's an idiot, thought Kyūsō.

Back then, footwear was sold in shabby roadside huts. Old men and young men down on their luck would be taken in and given jobs as gatekeepers and allowed to make and sell footwear on the side. The idea of a scholar and a samurai making his living in such a way was shocking, especially to a man like Kyūsō with a strong sense of propriety. Kyūsō believed that every man had his place, and that it was the appointed mission of a scholar to serve his country and give others peace of mind. To earn money by selling footwear meant looking out for one's own interest, improper behavior for a man of Confucian virtue. Then how to explain away the contradiction that he himself was living on a stipend taken from the earnings of common people, the sort who toiled at making and selling sandals? "Benevolence seeks the happiness of all, but selfish interest seeks only one's own happiness," he would argue. "It is better for society to have a benevolent man concerned with the happiness of all in a position of authority. Just as clouds rise and mud sinks, the order of people's place in society follows natural laws."

But Tōri had come to see this reasoning as sophistry. Master and pupil could come to no understanding.

"I have no intention of criticizing anyone else," said Tōri. "But I want to earn my living by my own efforts. I don't think it's right to receive a penny from anyone. This is how I want to live my life." He looked Kyūsō straight in the eye as he spoke. His eyes were clear. There was something erect and immovable in him.

Kyūsō yielded. "I won't bring it up again. Do as you please." He added, "You are a man of benevolence whose color can't be altered. Whether those around you turn black or white, you stay the same, and yet you quarrel with no one. You are a marvel."

Later on, Kyūsō would describe Tōri this way: "A man who was stubborn and unyielding, who didn't harp and wasn't quarrelsome, who could be ground fine without becoming thin and steeped without turning black." He also thought Tōri was like "a hard jewel." Most precious stones, if kicked around and rolled over rough terrain, lose their luster, but Tōri showed no sign whatever of such chafing. The difficulties he endured served only to burnish the luster of his spirit. A far cry from Ogyū Sorai, Kyūsō thought. In his opinion, Sorai's success, coming after his youthful struggles, had gone to his head.

"Let me tell you one final thing," said Kyūsō. "You mustn't give up your poetry. Don't cling to rhetoric at poetry's expense. Poetry that is overly concerned with rhetoric loses grace and becomes an exercise in logic. If it arises from the emotions, it has grace and will. You must remember this. Poetry that comes from the emotions conveys the will of Heaven and strikes the hearts of all. Nothing is more noble and beautiful than to live as a human being and leave a legacy of poetry."

Taking these words to heart, Tōri left Kanazawa behind.

Nakane Tōri was a heretical Confucian. Despite having won the approval of Muro Kyūsō, the finest Confucian scholar in the land, he declared that he could not in good conscience accept a stipend for pursuing scholarship and fled, turning his back on the prospect of becoming a career Confucian scholar in the service of the million-koku Kaga Domain.

His friends were scornful. "What a fool! How does he expect to feed himself?" Some of them were seriously worried and tried to track him down, but no one knew where he had gone. How could they have known that he was sitting in a squalid row house at Hatchōbori in Edo, seeing no one and scarcely sleeping as he sat covered in lice, reading day and night? Just as he had done in Kanazawa, twice a day he would come out of his trance, eat something, and relieve himself. When that was over, he would begin again to read. He scarcely seemed human; he was more like a windup doll.

One day, one of the row house tenants went up to him and asked why he read so many books. Tōri slowly looked up. "I read to fulfill my life. I'm so greedy that when I'm not reading I lose all sense of myself, wanting to eat good food and worrying that my money will run out. But really, it isn't right, reading books for sheer pleasure. I need to reflect more. People who can improve their character simply by reading are wonderful. But at the very least, reading should enable people to feel ashamed when they do something wrong. It's not right to read for pleasure the way I do."

After a while his provisions began to run out. Finally his rice bin was nearly empty. Death by starvation loomed.

He had two possible benefactors: Hosoi Kōtaku in Hongō, and Egan at Renkōji. If either of those men knew he was back in the city, they would undoubtedly be happy to take him in. But he was determined not to ask for help or rely on the kindness of others. He kept on reading.

I won't die right away, he thought. I'll just drink water and read.

Strangely, once he began reading with the knowledge that he might die, all his concern vanished. Reading was after all enjoyable. "Some drink water with pleasure; others wear brocade in distress," he mused. Life could be enjoyable even if one had only water to drink, and brocade robes were no barrier to misfortune.

Still, Tōri couldn't just lie down and die. He had a younger brother to think of. He came from a large family. When they had all gathered around his father's deathbed, the family circle had included four younger brothers and an elder sister, but a series of deaths had left him with just one sister and one brother. His sister, a woman of strong character, was married to a petty bureaucrat in Uraga. She was looking after their mother, so he had no concerns about either of them, but his lone surviving brother was so inept at getting on in the world, even in Tōri's eyes, that he was worrying.

The brother had a fine Confucian-style name, Toshinori, but he was so slow of speech and so close-mouthed that he earned little and barely managed to pay his rent. He lived in Kamakura on the edge of starvation.

One day something made Tōri scrape up the few remaining grains of rice at the bottom of his bin and set off for Kamakura. From then on he and his brother sold geta, wooden clogs, by the gateway to Tsurugaoka Hachiman Shrine. They gathered driftwood from Yuigahama Beach, carved it into clogs, and lined them up at the side of the approach to the shrine to sell to worshipers.

Until the fourteenth century, Japanese people customarily removed their footwear at the entrance to the sacred precincts of a temple or shrine and went in barefoot, so as not to pollute the grounds. The tradition persisted into the seventeenth and eighteenth centuries, as devout worshipers would frequently change to fresh footwear at the gate. This made the entrance to a temple or shrine a good place to sell footwear.

When Tōri first came up with the idea, his brother had immediately made a face. Selling footwear by the side of the road was the most despised occupation of that era.

"You're a learned man," Toshinori said in protest. "Why don't you become a doctor?"

He had a point. In any case, it was inconceivable that someone with enough education to peruse medical books should be hawking geta by the side of the road. You could search not just in Kamakura but in all Kantō, except Edo, and never find anyone as learned as Tōri. Besides, their father had been a doctor. If Tōri opened a practice, people were sure to flock to his door. Toshinori's suggestion made perfect sense.

But Tōri was firm. "I can't cure disease," he protested. "That much I'm certain of. If I opened a practice, yes, our lives would be easier, but it's deceitful to make people pay for medicine that won't do them any good."

His brother, who didn't have a deceitful bone in his body, nodded. And so the two of them began to sell geta. Those made by amateurs don't fetch a very high price. The brothers made them with care, but were taken advantage of by customers who bargained the price down to practically nothing. They barely got by. Selling one pair allowed them to eat that day. But during a spell of rainy weather they sold nothing, had nothing to eat, and were forced to endure hunger pains.

In time word got around: "There's a weird fellow who reads Chinese classics while he sells geta." Curiosity brought customers their way. Sitting by the side of the road in thin clothes while the cold winds blew left the brothers frozen in body and spirit, but finally they were able to afford a steady diet of rice porridge.

Around then a neighbor in the same row house came down with a nasty cough. Eventually he became bed-ridden. He couldn't afford millet rice, let alone a doctor's fee. At first other occupants of the house would cook rice for him, but they were all poor and lacked the means to care for him indefinitely. Soon, sadly, they began to keep their distance, only listening with pity to the sound of that hacking cough.

Tōri felt driven to do something. One day he made some porridge, took it to the man, and tried to spoon-feed him. The man, however, wouldn't eat. He opened hollow eyes and looked at Tōri. "I have no money," he said, "so I can't live long anyway. You eat this instead of me. I hear you used to be a priest. When I die, read a sutra for me and pray for my salvation."

Tōri was shocked. I can't let this man die, he thought.

He went straight home, gathered together his clothing and books, and set about tying them up in *furoshiki* cloths. His brother asked him what he was doing.

"That sick man is dying, but if he just had some medicine, his life could be saved. I'm going to pawn my clothes and my library to raise money."

"You mustn't do that! Sell my clothes if you want, I don't care. But you've spent the last ten years copying those books. Surely you don't have to go to such extremes to help a stranger." Toshinori tried desperately to stop him, unable to imagine how his brother could live without his books.

Tōri was unyielding. "A human life is more precious than any book," he declared, and went ahead and pawned all his possessions to save the man.

The Conduct of Tōri Sensei, a posthumous tribute from Tōri's followers, contains this passage: "A man who happened to live near him became ill. He was so poor that he could not afford medicine. To help him, Sensei pawned his entire collection of books and all his clothes."

The small room once buried in books now stood empty. With nothing to read, Tōri spent his nights gazing out the window at the moon. He sat quietly on the frayed tatami mats, bathed in moonlight.

"The room's bigger now, isn't it?" said his brother. "That man says he owes you his life, but when you think about it, we may be in his debt, too. He gave us the opportunity to triumph over greed. I've decided to look at it that way."

"I agree," said Tōri. "The purpose of learning is to draw closer to the true path, not to accumulate books. Even the words of Master Confucius are, you might say, a finger."

"A finger?"

Tōri pointed at the moon outside the window. "Without a finger to direct our gaze, we would see nothing but the interior of this shabby room. This would become our heaven and earth. But beyond the tip of this finger is the vast sky and the beautiful moon. The words of Master Confucius are a finger pointing us to the beauty of the moon. All we need to do is look."

Toshinori was struck dumb.

"We mustn't wear out our spirits and lose precious time by pursuing useless words, seeking to read what is unreadable and understand what is abstruse. I was in danger of mistaking the finger for the moon. The Four Books and Five Classics are only fingers. What matters is the moon beyond."

He who sees the moon can forget the pointing finger: this way of thinking was radical. Hardly anyone in this era dared to suggest that the true value of Confucian thought lay outside the classical texts and that once you had laid hold of that value, you could walk away from the books that had served as guides.

So Tōri sold all his possessions. When he had made sure that the former invalid was fully recovered, he left Kamakura. The brothers agreed that if they stayed on, the man might find their presence oppressive, and so they moved. Using their connections, they became guards of the town gate near Benkei Bridge in Edo. Such guards commonly made and sold footwear, but their amateur handiwork attracted little attention in a city filled with professional geta craftsmen.

Somehow the penniless brothers learned to weave bamboo sheaths into sandals, which they hung from the eaves of their guard-hut and sold. The place where they lived now was a hole in the wall about the size of two tatami mats, though of course they had no such luxury as tatami. Wind and rain blew in through the cracks. They slept curled up together.

Tōri would always wake up at the same time every morning and go to a bamboo grove to gather sheaths. During the day he would carefully weave them into sandals and close the gate at ten at night. The bamboo sandals sold fairly well. When he had saved enough money, he ordered more books to read.

In time, neighborhood children came by and asked him to teach them to read and write. He wrote with a stick on the ground to teach them their letters. Soon they were calling him "Bamboo Sandal Sensei."

One little boy, a sweet, round-cheeked tyke of about three, gave him cause for concern. His father had brought him to the neighboring row house, holding him tightly in his arms. The boy was clearly motherless. The father had to go out to earn a living and so couldn't look after him; instead he asked a woman living there to do the job for a fee. She put on a smile and said yes. But her reputation in the neighborhood was unsavory. Her mouth was like a slash from ear to ear, and she was avaricious. People called her a "she-wolf" behind her back. At first she looked after the boy as if he were her own child, and people were surprised—could the she-wolf have a maternal side after all? But alas, the boy's cheeks grew more sunken by the day. Tōri asked someone about the situation, and the answer was sharp: "That woman's a bad character. Once she got a generous handout for child support, she stopped feeding the kid. All she ever wanted was to get her hands on the money."

Tōri wanted to do something to help the boy. But to the cunning she-wolf, the boy was a source of cash, one she had no intention of letting go. Seeing Tōri's concern, she only abused him more harshly. If Tōri had had access to a great deal of money, things might have been different, but he was penniless and frustrated. In the daytime he kept watch at the gate while also keeping an eye on the situation. Late at night, he and his brother would weave sandals and talk about it.

Holding a cord of bamboo between his toes as he weaved, Tōri said, "Nobody feeds that boy when he's hungry. Nobody gives him water when he's thirsty. Nobody holds him by the hand, and he goes to sleep alone. He's too little to be able to say much, and he can't do anything, so he thrashes about and cries, but that only makes her beat him. He seems to understand that. The poor thing cries and cries, trying not to make a sound."

"How can people be so cruel?" wondered Toshinori. "When they see how weak he is, the other kids gather round and gang up on him, bullying him and making fun of him. They spit in his face and twist his arm, drag him around by his hair, scratch him, and make him vomit. They make a game out of getting him to shriek and cry, and that woman does nothing to stop them. She joins right in, laughing. What's really unforgivable is that when the father comes by she pretends to dote on the boy, holding him and caressing him and talking sweetly. 'Look, it's Daddy!' she purrs. 'Come on, smile, talk to him.' She's crafty."

"I saw that, too. The boy's starved for love. He doesn't want to be ill-treated, he wants any scrap of affection. So when she picks him up and holds him, even though her love isn't real, he smiles and talks bravely to his father. A starving man will eat anything, they say, and a thirsty man will drink anything. When I look at the boy, I see the sadness of desperation."

"I wonder if the father has any idea what's going on."

"I think he does," said Tōri. "He sees how thin his son is; he must know the situation. He just doesn't say a word. Probably he wants his brief visits to be some solace for the boy. He gazes at him with a smile. The boy looks into his father's eyes and seems to understand his sorrow. 'Daddy's here!' he shouts. 'Daddy's here!' His joy at such moments only reflects the pain he endures the rest of the time. It's sad."

Toshinori was silent.

"So the father hugs his son, feeds him and gives him something to drink, does whatever the child wants and sees that he enjoys their time together to the fullest before he goes away." Tōri's voice caught. "When he leaves, to avoid a scene he doesn't tell the boy he's going. He gives him sweets or a doll and then always says, 'Daddy's going to the bathroom' or 'Daddy's going next door.' The boy smiles and says 'Okay, Daddy,' and then the father is gone. The moment he is through the gate, the bullies come back and tear the treats and doll from the little boy's hands, so he ends up with nothing. The poor thing calls for his father, sobbing, until his tears dry and he falls asleep. When he wakes up, he starts to sob again. It's a living hell."

This tale of child abuse from three hundred years ago has been handed down through some of Tōri's few surviving writings. I wrote the above while deciphering the account Tōri wrote in Chinese. His prose is hauntingly sad. As I read, the words engraved themselves on my mind. Japanese people have written in Chinese for a thousand years, but how many have seen into the heart of a child the way Tōri did and left such a feeling description in Chinese? It makes me wonder if Japanese scholars of Confucianism and the native branch of scholarship called *kokugaku*, national studies, ever really achieved the philosopher's goal of benevolence at all.

Concerning what became of the abused boy, Tōri writes, "I was unable to find out any more." At some point the child disappeared. In the Edo period, barely half of all children, however cherished, survived to adulthood. The fate of a three-year-old who suffered continuous abuse, his body covered in bruises and scars, was a foregone conclusion.

For a while afterwards, Tōri lived staring into the void. Why, he wondered, had he devoted himself to learning? He was agitated. Unanswerable questions came and went in his mind. He lay down in his cramped room and stretched out as far as he could. He had already finished reading the new books he'd acquired after pawning his library. Then he realized there was one more that he hadn't yet read: *The Complete Works of Wang Yangming*. A sympathetic friend had brought it over for him, but he had never opened it. He had a reason for not wishing to read that particular book: Muro Kyūsō, his former teacher, had warned him to stay away from Wang Yangming and instead take Zhu Xi's orthodox school of Neo-Confucianism as his model.

"Until the middle of the Ming dynasty," Kyūsō had explained, "Chinese learning was correct. But then along came someone named Wang Yangming, preaching *liangzhi* or 'innate knowledge of the good.' He began saying things like, 'Don't think about difficult things. Follow the innate knowledge that lies within you.' But the path of learning consists in mastering principles one by one. If you are going to become aware of principles naturally, without such efforts, then you might as well do *zazen* meditation. His theory of 'innate knowledge' is false Buddhism trying to pass itself off as Confucianism."

Kyūsō had dismissed Wang Yangming as "a follower of twisted Zen," and argued fiercely against his teaching. At the time, Tōri had been fed up with Zen, so this line of reasoning had satisfied him. That's why even when he finally took the book in hand to read, he did so, according to the record, "lying down"—that is, in a posture that failed to show proper respect. But as he read on, he began to feel as if mist were clearing before his eyes. When he came to the theories concerning *zhizhi gewu*, "extend knowledge and investigate things," and *zhixing heyi*, "unity of knowledge and action," he could scarcely take his eyes off the page. He jumped up, composed himself, and sat down in the proper posture. "The heart of Confucian instruction is in this book," he marveled. "Why did it take me so long to read it?"

From then on, Tōri devoured Wang Yangming's words. Ideas that had been half-formed in his mind took clear shape. For decades he had devoted himself to reading, but never before had he had an almost transcendent experience of this nature.

The classic *Book of Rites* contains a chapter called "Great Learning" wherein Confucius sets forth eight steps for the superior man to take: investigate things, extend knowledge, make one's thoughts sincere, rectify the mind, cultivate the self, regulate the family, order the state, make the world tranquil. The basis of all these tasks is given as *gewu*, a compound that Zhu Xi glosses as "investigate things." He interprets it as meaning "to seek out and understand the fundamental principles (*li*) of things, that is, the natural principles that inhere in all creation." But as far as Tōri could tell, Wang Yangming's interpretation was completely different and compellingly fresh. Wang Yangming glosses the compound as "rectify things" and, unlike Zhu Xi, clearly elucidates the fundamental question, "What are 'things'?"

Tōri understood what he read to mean: Zhu Xi speaks of seeking out and understanding the fundamental principles of things, yet the consciousness that regards things has no absolute existence apart from them. Things and the mind that observes them are one and the same, not disparate entities. Therefore, we should live with the awareness that the self and "things" are fundamentally one.

As he read on to the end of *Instructions for Practical Living*, he came upon this passage.

> Man is the mind of the universe. At heart heaven, earth, and all things are one body with me. Does anyone's suffering or bitterness fail to cause me pain? ... Regard others as oneself, regard the country as one's family. Heaven, earth, and all things form one body.

He rephrased it. "Consider that man is the mind of the universe. Heaven, earth, and all things are a harmonious whole. If people anywhere are suffering, their pain is mine. Humans like me, animals, and plants are born of the universe, and in time all die and disappear into the universe. All are basically one and the same. Thinking in this state of mind, nothing in this world is unconnected to me."

It was definitely true. Many people might find such thinking hard to swallow, but Tōri was not one of them. If, as Wang Yangming said, people were at heart one with the universe, then they must be born with a mind capable of sensing it. That must be what Mencius meant by *liangzhi*, "innate knowledge." Then just as a bird carries food to its young and a mother gives milk to her child, a spirit of warmth would inevitably be cultivated in all people, however long it might take. Tōri's mission, as someone who had read extensively, was to teach that truth to people in his words and deeds. He was amazed and heartened to think that two centuries before him, a man had been engrossed in such thoughts.

Little by little Tōri began to teach. At first he would simply answer a question if asked, and teach those who sought him out, but compared to the days when he avoided contact with people, something had clearly changed. He was just about to turn thirty.

In time, he acquired a follower. A man named Kozuka Shimpo came to him from the village of Ueno in Shimotsuke Province (present-day Tochigi Prefecture). However he may have heard of Tōri, he would come to his hut, listen to him talk, and leave with a beaming face. He was a pleasant man and fond of looking after others. After a while he declared that he wanted his landlord to hear Tōri speak, and took Tōri to meet him at a great stable for post horses run by a man named Takagi. The landlord, a lover of learning, begged Tōri to stay and lecture on the classics.

And so after nearly ten years of living in a tiny hut, Tōri went back to a proper house with tatami mats on the floor. However, he soon left. He never liked to stay long in one place. People said of him, "Soot never collects in his chimney."

Around this time, more and more people began to appreciate Tōri's virtues. He rented a small place at the gate to Fukagawa Hachiman Shrine in Edo where again he sold handmade bamboo sandals but also increasingly gave lectures.

Some of his pupils would come later than the agreed-on time, but he never seemed to mind; he never once scolded anyone for being late, although he himself was punctual. People observed humorously that his daily activities were as regular as the progress of the heavenly bodies in their spheres.

In spring, Tōri went for walks outside the city. He loved flowers, especially peach blossom, which produced luscious fruit that was a boon to life. A friend of his named Muga would invite him on outings to peach orchards. This Muga was another eccentric fellow. Here is how they met.

One day, as Tōri was selling sandals, he was addressed by a fortune-teller. When Tōri asked his name, he answered only "Muga" (Non-self) and gave no surname.

"Non-self is a strange name. How did you come by it?"

"Confucius said we must renounce four things. Do not conjecture, do not make arbitrary decisions, do not be fanatical, have no ego. The last renunciation is the most difficult. That's why I call myself Non-self."

They became fast friends. Tōri rented a room on the second floor over an oil merchant's shop, and he and this virtuous recluse who made his living as a fortune-teller would walk together among the blossoming trees in the eastern suburbs of Edo. Blossom-viewers spread feasts beneath the trees, enjoying fine sake and food. But Muga and Tōri, having no money, could only look and walk on by. It was Tōri's custom to murmur poetry as he walked, and so he began to do so. He improvised the following poem in Chinese:

The eastern fields are full of gaiety

The valley breezes are fragrant
Here some drink wine
There some eat meat
I am already sated, already drunk
My mind is full of joy.

When Muga heard this, he laughed. "That's a funny thing to say. Those people are enjoying themselves drinking. Why should that make you happy?"

"It does, though. Simply empty yourself. Then I become the other and the other becomes me; there are no boundaries in feelings either; there is no longer anything that isn't mine. If you are obsessed with yourself, you grow concerned over wealth and poverty, fame and insignificance, long life and early death, happiness and unhappiness, birth and death, fortune and misfortune, honor and shame. You end up suffering. If you empty yourself, then we are all the same. Nurturing others properly, stopping fights, forbidding violence, doing away with bullying, and all such actions aren't really done for others but are ways of healing one's own illness."

"Yes, but it takes a sage to be able to think like that."

"Not at all. There's no reason to limit such thinking to sages. Shouldn't we all try to be like that? Everyone should do what they can to polish the gem in their own mind. Some are large and some are small. Maybe we can't all polish a gem as large as that of a sage, but even a small one, if polished, will sparkle. To polish the gem in one's mind—that, to me, is our task in life."

Muga looked startled. He walked through the peach-fragrant air in silence for a while before asking, "How can we do it?"

"I have a notion about that, but I can't put it into words."

Muga looked at him inquiringly.

"It might come down to humility. Putting others first, oneself last. If one kept that always in mind, it might be possible to renounce the self and attain benevolence."

Muga was delighted to hear this, and promptly changed his name to Kensai, using the character for "humility." So the story goes.

Some four years later, Tōri moved to Sano in the province of Shimotsuke. He went because his follower, Kozuka Shimpo, begged him: "Please let the people in my hometown hear you lecture on *Instructions for Practical Living*." A retreat called Deigetsuan (Mud-Moon Hermitage) was built for him in the village of Ueno, and he lived there and lectured on Wang Yangming at Kozuka's house. Though the house wasn't small, so many people flocked to hear him that the parlor filled to overflowing.

Tōri's lectures were eminently practical. He prioritized ease of understanding and didn't embellish his speech. He spoke in familiar terms, using analogies, and so although he spoke of lofty matters his lectures didn't seem difficult. Those listening in his audience could reach understanding on their own.

A boy named Sudō Atsushi walked a long distance to hear one of these lectures. Tōri made these remarks about reading: "There is a certain way of reading a book. The reader must decide what the important part is and make up his mind to read that part with great care. Suppose you went sightseeing in the city and saw only little gates and eateries, and went home without having seen the castle or palace. Could you truly say you had seen the city? Reading is just the same. Searching for the truth, the Way, is like searching for food while you are starving. You have no food, so you have no time to waste wandering around unnecessary places. In order to find the Way, you need to go straight to the most important part of the book and read that."

Most Confucian lectures of that time consisted less in expounding the Way than in explaining phrases in the texts. The teacher would go through a book phrase by phrase from the beginning, and so earn his pay. But Tōri declared that it wasn't necessary to read the whole book. This evidently made a huge impression on Sudō, for thirty years later, he recalled the lecture clearly.

Tōri's words had depth. "The teachings of Confucius are not difficult in the least. You must understand only one thing." All anyone needed to know, he said, was the principle that heaven and earth and all things are one.

"All Confucian learning can be boiled down to a single character: *jin*, benevolence. *Jin* is the mind of unity with heaven, earth, and all things. It includes justice, courtesy, wisdom, and sincerity. Certainly at first glance the myriad of things in the universe appear to be so various that they could never be one. But please consider this. Everything in the universe has come into existence through the energy of the universe. In that sense, everything is one. When sunlight and rain pour down from the sky, plant life grows on the mountains and crops grow in the fields. Birds and beasts and human beings are the result. Everyone is my flesh and bone, from my parents and children to my brothers and sisters, and all those yet to be born. Sun and moon, rain and dew, mountain and river, plants and animals, fish and turtles—all are one and all are me. That's how grand Confucian thought is, and how simple.

"Even though I say these things," he concluded, "I myself am a nobody. I read these theories over and over and teach them to others, but I am like a frog in a well that knows nothing of the ocean. Try as I might to attain the broad mind that sees no division between the self and others, I have little success and suffer torments. I am exactly like a dog or a cat going around and around in circles chasing its own tail. I know that it's because I think constantly of myself."

For nearly thirty years, Tōri continued to live in Sano. At one point he returned to Uraga for three years to take care of his dying mother. He was present at her deathbed, spent three years tending her grave, and then returned to Sano, where he taught and was revered. He never married, but circumstances compelled him to become the guardian of his niece.

His brother, Toshinori, had become independent after Tōri moved to Sano and in his mid-forties finally took a wife. In due time a daughter, Yoshiko, was born, but all too soon the mother died. Left with a newborn to care for, Toshinori was desperate to provide her with sustenance. He had no milk to offer, nor could he afford a wet-nurse. He had to go around begging when the baby cried, asking some other man's wife to provide milk. But a newborn can't drink much at once, so she was soon hungry and crying again. Each time this happened, he had to get up and seek more milk for her, wandering the streets late at night. He came by so often that people were put off and finally withdrew their help. He tried elsewhere, but again was turned down. At this rate, Yoshiko would die. In desperation, he and his aged mother-in-law together heated some gruel and spoon-fed the infant, saving her life.

After Yoshiko turned three, another difficulty arose. Her grandmother, worn out from caring for her, took sick and died. Toshinori had to make some money, and so he was forced to leave his daughter with an old woman in the neighborhood. He worked as hard as he could, but couldn't earn enough to pay for her care. The woman stopped looking after her properly. Like the boy who'd been left with the she-wolf, Yoshiko began to waste away. Toshinori walked through the winter winds all the way from Uraga in Sagami Province, a distance of nearly 125 miles, eating nothing. When he arrived in Sano he collapsed in tears.

"Brother, forgive me. I have nowhere else to turn."

"Why didn't you bring her with you!" Tōri shouted, enraged.

Toshinori went back to Uraga to fetch his daughter, then turned around and carried her on his back to Sano. When they arrived, she was breathing, but her condition was piteous. Whatever she may have been fed, she suffered from diarrhea for days on end. Her belly was swollen like a drum, her scalp was scabby, and she was covered in lice. Tōri took over the care of his dying niece, and Toshinori went home to Sagami.

Tōri had by then built up a life in Sano. The villagers had all pitched in to construct a retreat for him. Called Chishōan, "Knowledge among the Pines," it was a small thatched hut measuring 15 feet north and south and 16 feet east and west with poor windows and no proper entrance. Here he raised Yoshiko and taught the villagers.

When the weather was fine, Mt. Fuji was visible in the direction of Sagami. Tōri would dandle the little girl on his knees and tell her, "That's where you're from, over there."

Around this time Tōri would do "wall writing" for the benefit of those who came to his academy. He wrote things like this:

"The lumberjack climbs mountains, the fisherman floats on the sea. Let each enjoy his calling."

"Some drink water with pleasure, others wear brocade in distress."

Tōri was now fifty-three. Death might come at any time. If he were to die, what would become of Yoshiko? Left alone, would she not be engulfed in life's ceaseless waves of sadness? As he mulled this prospect, words came to his mind. "Wait for the rising moon. Don't chase after scattered flowers." He added this to his wall writing.

On February 7, 1765, Tōri died. He was seventy-one years old. He left behind no possessions to speak of, nor any great collection of writings. A single volume, entitled *New Tiles*, emerged from a cloth wrapper. When his followers opened the book, they found an account, written in elegant Chinese prose, of his niece Yoshiko's background and the details of her coming to Sano. In words simple enough for a four-year-old girl to chew on and appreciate, the essence of his thought was laid out. The brilliant poet departed this world leaving behind only this work. Here and there the pages were decorated in his own hand with colorful drawings of little birds and animals.

After that, Tōri was all but forgotten. Those he had taught scrambled to find other writings of his, and when they heard of any they would run to claim them, even scrap paper. They had little luck. Finally they managed to publish *The Posthumous Works of Tōri*, but only a few copies were printed. Repeated attempts to reprint the book came to nothing. A hundred years after Tōri died, *Additional Works by Tōri* was published. Today the most complete collection of his works is *Annotated Posthumous Writings of Tōri*, edited by Kumekawa Shin'ya. The charitable work of a dedicated man, it was printed privately in small numbers. (While I was writing this life of Tōri, not one library in Tokyo could furnish me with a copy.)

But the thinker Tōri did live. In an age before the existence of atoms and molecules was known, he understood intuitively that we and the universe are one, and he applied this truth to how people should live their lives. Such a man unquestionably lived and breathed in a small village of Sano.

For two and a half centuries his memory has lived on in that village. When I went to Sano, I asked directions from an old man I happened to meet. "Tōri Sensei? He lived in that temple over there," he said, and graciously showed me the way. Then, as if revealing something of immense importance, he added, "He was a truly great man." His tone was soft. The sound of that calm voice lingers in my ears, unforgettable.

3. Ōtagaki Rengetsu

(1791–1875)

What is the source of human gentleness? Contemplating the life of the Buddhist nun Ōtagaki Rengetsu (1791–1875), a brilliant poet and potter, I can't help asking myself this question.

Rengetsu was by no means well born. She never met her father, and whether she had even a single encounter with her mother is unclear. Nothing can be said with certainty about the identity of either parent. Where even to begin looking for information to use in writing about her origins is a puzzle. This much, however, is beyond doubt: on the last day of January in 1788, a great fire broke out in Kyoto, a conflagration said to be the worst in three centuries. This fire had a considerable connection with Rengetsu's entrance into the world. Flames that raged for three days and three nights set in motion the events that would lead to her birth.

It all began, the story goes, with a marital spat. That morning in Dongurizushi, Miyagawa-machi, a husband and wife in a rear tenement on the eastern bank of the Kamo River got into a fight during which a charcoal brazier was overturned. That set off the fire. The couple's house burned instantly to the ground; high winds carried sparks across the river and fanned the flames, spreading them with ferocious speed. By evening Nijō Castle had burned down. During the night the ravenous fire approached and devoured the Imperial Palace. The emperor was whisked by palanquin into the forest at nearby Shimogamo Shrine for safety. This is what became known as the "Donguri Fire."

Kyoto has experienced many conflagrations, but none as destructive as this one. During the Ōnin War of 1467–1477, fires broke out at intervals and the havoc wrought was slow; the "Gun Fire" of 1864 that followed the Hamaguri Gate Rebellion, when anti-shogunate forces tried to seize control of the Imperial Palace, was not nearly so extensive. The Donguri Fire ravaged the city. Afterward, the pagoda of Tōji Temple could be seen from afar, and the great hall of Nishi Honganji Temple, which survived thanks to the frenzied firefighting of a brigade of monks, loomed dimly amid the ashes. Crowds of people whose homes had burned down began camping out in the dry riverbed of the Kamo River. It was fiercely cold. Survivors could only sob away their sorrows, awaiting alms.

An eerie song became popular in the burned-out wasteland. Children bounced balls and chanted:

> The Year of the Monkey at the start of the year
> The king lost his home and people died oh dear
> Tōji pagoda, off that way
> Honganji Temple, over this way
> Ninety-nine thousand houses in town
> Eighty-eight thousand burned to the ground
> Chestnut trees twenty years used to grow
> Now there's lumber wherever you go.

Chestnut trees that had been growing for twenty years were cut down to rebuild the capital. The circumstances that led to Rengetsu's birth came about during this time of rebuilding.

When the Imperial Palace goes up in flames, say people in Kyoto, love children are born to important men. After the palace and the daimyo residences burn down, it's time to rebuild; high-ranking samurai pour into town and in their off hours go out to have fun—and that's how love children get born, as any young Kyotoite would tell you.

Kyoto women are adept at the shamisen and dancing. Some merchant families used to have their daughters undergo more extensive training so they might entertain at banquets and find a wealthy patron. After the fire, everyone lost their means of making a living, so even proper young ladies seemingly far from the world of geisha ended up turning professional. It's said there were easily more than a thousand of them.

Rengetsu's mother was one such woman. She performed in the pleasure district of Sanbongi, near the Imperial Palace, an area patronized by the wealthy and powerful. Various daimyo would invariably hold meetings there when resident in Kyoto, and members of the court nobility dropped by as well. Sometimes imperial princes would even pay clandestine visits. Patrons were mostly men of the world, known for being generous spenders.

Shortly after the Donguri Fire, a young samurai of singular good looks began frequenting Sanbongi. He was a member of the Tōdō clan in Tsu Domain and had come to Kyoto from Iga Ueno. Whether his name was Shinshichirō or Kinshichi is impossible to determine.

In the past, literary critic Sugimoto Hidetarō tried to find out the identity of Rengetsu's real father, and I undertook the same task, digging into archives. All I had to go on was this statement from the child of Rengetsu's wet-nurse: "She was the love child of a lord named Tōdō Kinshichirō, head of the castle in Iga Ueno."

A single volume in Tokyo's National Diet Library contains a detailed genealogy of the Tōdō clan. It was privately printed, and is called *Tōdōsei shokatō kafushū* (Genealogies of various families with the surname Tōdō), edited by Hayashi Izumi. No Tōdō Kinshichirō is listed there; instead I found a Tōdō Kinshichi and a Tōdō Shinshichirō. Rengetsu was born in January 1791, so I needed to track down a man surnamed Tōdō who was in Kyoto on business around March 1790, but I couldn't find anything definite.

Tōdō Kinshichi was a divisional commander with a stipend of three thousand koku, and Tōdō Shinshichirō was his younger brother-in-law. They were both divisional commanders and chief retainers in the same domain, but I was unable to find any record of a 1790 visit to Kyoto by either of them. One Tōdō Kyūbei did go to Kyoto in November of that year, but he was probably not Rengetsu's father. The only conclusion I can draw is that "Tōdō Kinshichirō" was a misrepresentation of either Kinshichi or Shinshichirō. Someone may have misheard the latter name. In any case, Rengetsu's father was apparently someone in the Tōdō clan. In that case, she had an illustrious lineage.

Tōdō Shinshichirō received a hereditary stipend of five thousand koku.

His true name was Yoshikiyo, and he was descended from Shinshichirō Yoshikatsu, cousin of Tōdō Takatora (1556–1630), the first lord of Tsu. Yoshikatsu became known for his bravery in the battle of Sekigahara in 1600, when he attacked and defeated Ōtani Yoshitsugu (1558–1600; also known by his court title, Gyōbu). He fought for Takatora without thought of personal gain. When Takatora attempted to reward him with a hereditary stipend of ten thousand koku, he wouldn't accept it. Takatora then raised the amount to twenty thousand, but again Yoshikatsu declined, riling his lord so that he ended up with five thousand koku.

It should be added that haiku master Matsuo Bashō was originally a retainer in Shinshichirō's family, which was known for its refined taste. Bashō served as a cook in their kitchens.

I will continue the story on the assumption that Tōdō Shinshichirō was Rengetsu's father.

The Tōdō family residence in Kyoto, built at Shijō Horikawa on the site of the old residence of Lord Furuta Oribe (1544–1615; a daimyo and tea master for whom Oribe ware was named) was among those destroyed in the fire. Taki Yoemon, the Tōdō family's official representative in Kyoto, lost no time in scraping through the ashes and fencing off the property, but six months went by before the surrounding long house and gate were restored, and still more time was needed to rebuild the mansion. Many retainers from Ise Iga were in Kyoto, Shinshichirō possibly among them. Taki may have taken it upon himself to entertain the bored young man who held an important position in the domain. As the family scion, he would have been treated with great deference.

And so Shinshichirō was escorted to Sanbongi.

The pleasure houses of Sanbongi were a little unusual. There were no in-house entertainers; rather, the establishment would send for local geisha. As soon as the customer was seated, before the meal was served a waitress would ask which geisha he preferred. Overriding Shinshichirō's protestation—"I'm no sophisticate"—she produced a list of geisha names and advised him, "You should send for this one."

Eventually the door slid open and in stepped a comely geisha. Her eyes met his. That was the start of it all.

Shinshichirō saw her again and again. It is safe to say that he fell in love. The twenty-four-old young lord was married to a woman of the Tōdō clan who was carrying his child—but his passion overcame his good sense. The geisha responded to his passion and conceived a child, the future Rengetsu. This happened in the spring of 1790.

One day Shinshichirō revealed to the geisha that he was the child of a concubine. His mother had lived for years alongside his father's true wife. Her family was from Kanazawa, but she was descended from a mere rear vassal, the retainer of a retainer. From the time he was small, he had seen all too clearly how out of place his mother, a concubine of low birth, was made to feel.

When he learned the geisha was pregnant with his child, Shinshichirō was torn. The Tōdō residence was nearly rebuilt, and work on the palace was also progressing. When the reconstruction was finished and his time in Kyoto was up, he would have to return to Iga. What to do with this woman and her child? What may have subsequently passed between the two of them, no one knows. All that is clear is that they treated the new life they had created— Rengetsu—as a nuisance.

Shinshichirō turned to a man named Yamazaki Tsune'emon, a samurai serving Chion'in Temple. The son of a farmer in Tottori, Inaba Province, he had come to the capital and against heavy odds managed to become a temple retainer. Tsune'emon was thirty-five, just ten years older than Shinshichirō, but far lower in status. He was a *sangoku-san* or "three koku man," as low-paid samurai in the service of court nobles or head priests were called. Such men had one thin kimono to their name and in the bitter cold of winter would sometimes urinate on their feet to warm them. That's the sort of miserable lives they led, samurai or not.

The two men met through the game of go. Here the record is clear. Shinshichirō heard about Tsune'emon's skill at the game, for which he was well known, and several times asked to play against him. Tsune'emon's moves were supremely elegant. A leisurely game of go with this genial companion was a pleasant way to pass the time. Recalling this, Shinshichirō had a feeling that Tsune'emon would come to his aid—a casually self-centered way of thinking that was the hallmark of a feudal lord. It must have been in his blood.

"I was wondering if you could help me," ventured Shinshichirō, putting poor Tsune'emon immediately on the spot. "I got a woman pregnant. Take care of it for me. I'll see that there's something in it for you."

Out of the blue, this outrageous request landed in Tsune'emon's lap. What to do? As he folded his arms and thought it over, gradually he was overcome with pity—pity not for the young lord but for his unborn child. His next words came naturally: "All right. I'll take the child." This decision would cost him dearly. There could hardly be a greater imposition, after all.

By then the geisha's belly had swollen almost to the bursting point; the baby might pop out at any time. Once born, it would need milk, so Tsune'emon set out to find a wet-nurse. Since he worked at a temple and was of lowly status there, New Year's was his busiest time of year, from the ringing of the great temple bell on New Year's Eve through the first seven days of the new year. He had to work like a dog, running in circles to take care of all the temple business. In odd moments he searched for a woman who could feed the baby.

In those days, people believed that a wet-nurse needed to be a virtuous woman of good disposition. She would pass her traits to the infant along with her milk, it was thought, and have a determining influence on the child's character. Fortunately, he soon found someone: a married woman by the family name of Takahashi who lived on the north side of the street by the temple's old gate, just west of Kobori. She had recently given birth to a daughter and had plenty of milk to spare. She agreed to nurse another child.

Tsune'emon deftly finalized the arrangements before going to pick up the newborn child, who had been born at the hour of the tiger (four in the morning) on the eighth day of the New Year, 1791. He sprinted along the bank of the Kamo River to Sanbongi and saw the baby lying on a bed of straw, a jewel of a little girl.

"She was born on the eighth day of the New Year, a lucky day for sure," they said. The number eight was held to be lucky because of the spreading lines of the character it is written with (八), which seemed to bode well for the future. "And for a girl to be born at the hour of the tiger is a sign of valor, too!" Kyotoites were superstitious in this way, particularly concerning the zodiac. The pleasure quarters were full of theories about what was lucky or unlucky. A female born in the year of the tiger would grow up to devour her husband, people whispered in all seriousness, or be as strong-minded as any man. Such superstition explains why even though the name of the baby's mother is unknown, we have an exact record of the year, month, day, and hour of her birth.

The next question was, what to call her? Tsune'emon thought it over and decided on the name Nobu, written with a character meaning "sincerity."

The baby's mother nursed her for ten days and then disappeared. However the match may have come about, she married into a samurai family in Kameyama, just one mountain away. And so Rengetsu started life abandoned by both father and mother.

From birth, she had an intelligent, almost masculine face. Her features were clear-cut, her eyes calm, her skin very fair. She seemed destined to become a rare beauty. Everyone agreed that they had never seen an infant with such an air of grace. They took turns holding her.

Tsune'emon, however, was troubled. However fine and intelligent her features, a girl was still a girl. How much better if she'd been a boy, he thought. A boy in her circumstances wouldn't face much difficulty in life. A boy, even if born to a concubine, could be raised as a member of the Tōdō family. After all, her father was a young lord with a stipend celebrated in local song: "Tōdō

Shinshichi and Gemba of Iga Ueno. They bind their hair with straw yet earn five thousand koku."

Tōdō Takatora started out as the governor of Anotsu in Ise Province, with an income of 320,000 koku, and became daimyo of present-day Tottori thanks to the battlefield actions of his cousins Shinshichirō Yoshikatsu and Gemba, both of whom oddly chose to bind their hair with straw in the manner of common foot soldiers. Banners aloft—Yoshikatsu's battle standard a dharma wheel, Gemba's a black streamer—they rushed the field, breaking through enemy lines and leading heroic charges. Both men ultimately fell in battle as a result of their desperate, life-or-death actions. Nobu's father was the sixth-generation descendant of the valiant Shinshichirō Yoshikatsu (memorialized in the song as "Shinshichi").

Whether that family history accounts for it who can say, but from the first, the infant's eyes shone with uncommon spirit. And yet she was every inch a girl.

Tsune'emon agreed to adopt her even though he was by no means confident that he could raise a child properly. He was employed at the temple but still had a hard time making ends meet. Many people in his situation wouldn't have thought twice about fleecing the young lord for child support, but Tsune'emon was a good-hearted, decent man.

Years ago on one life-changing day his farmer father had shown him an old family history. Sitting before a scroll labeled "Ōtagaki Family Genealogy," he'd listened to his father explain that they were descended from Ōtagaki the lord of Tajima, one of four 'Heavenly Kings' of the powerful Yamana clan. The Yamana had been one of four shogun families in the Muromachi period and house elders of the Ashikaga clan. At one time they had ruled a vast territory amounting to one sixth the area of Japan, so the family head had been known as "Lord One Sixth." Their distant ancestor had been lord of a castle, the remains of which still existed in Takeda, Tajima. If history had gone the right way, Tsune'emon himself could have been a daimyo. He learned these things with amazement.

The discovery of his family's prestigious roots was to have a profound effect on Tsune'emon's life. He and his wife had lost four infant sons in succession. When she conceived for the fifth time, something inside him snapped. "This life will never come again," he told her. "I don't want to end my days a nameless farmer. I'll go into service somewhere as a samurai, and when I get settled I'll send for you and the child." Vague dread, a sense that he was burdened by bad karma and that staying where he was would ensure the death of their next child, too, may have driven him to act. At any rate, off he went, leaving behind his pregnant wife and taking with him the family-tree scroll. He first searched for his ancestor's castle in the mountains. After visiting the ruins, before going on to Kyoto, he called on distant kinsmen in Tajima.

There is something almost comical about an obsession with ancient family history that would drive a man such actions. But in any case, he was mistaken about the name "Ōtagaki." It was properly written with a character meaning "grand," but perhaps because on the scroll the distinguishing middle stroke was missing, he believed that it was written with a similar character of the same pronunciation meaning "large." He always used the less impressive character to write his name, and so did Rengetsu. Her tombstone, as well as that of the family grave, is engraved with the wrong character.

When ordered to adopt the infant by the young Tōdō lord—who was indeed from a distinguished family tree—Tsune'emon reportedly responded, "How can a man such as myself, someone of no account, take on your princess?" (*The Collected Works of the Nun Rengetsu*) Yet he didn't have the heart to say no.

Only samurai were entitled to use surnames. The easiest way to become a samurai at the time was to go to Kyoto. The shogunate and domains rarely took on new samurai, but in the capital there were all sorts of impecunious authorities under the shogunate's thumb, including court nobles, hereditary Shinto priests, and temples with head priests of imperial lineage. Anyone taken on as retainer by one of these authorities was a bona fide samurai, if in name only. Such a person could have a surname and wear a *haori* and *hakama* over his kimono and carry two swords, but his stipend—if any—would be next to nothing. In fact, sometimes it worked the other way around: men paid good money to become retainers, providing impoverished Kyoto nobles with a source of spending money.

So Tsune'emon had gone to Kyoto and, after three years of painstaking effort, managed to became a *terazamurai*—a samurai performing administrative and other functions at a temple. Now he too could carry swords, but he could not yet use the name Ōtagaki. Chion'in Temple, having imperial connections, could not take on someone lacking any tie to the imperial household. Reluctantly, he agreed to be adopted into the Yamazaki family. Only then was he able to serve the temple. His joy at attaining samurai rank must have been halved, since he still yearned to restore the Ōtagaki family to samurai status. Though a farmer by birth without any true surname, he identified completely with the Ōtagaki name. In this he was typical of his time. Farmers throughout the land attached importance to having a family name and began looking back to distant ancestors and identifying with them as samurai, sometimes relocating to Kyoto to seek that status. This deep-seated shift in Tokugawa society would lead eventually to the earth-shaking Meiji Restoration of 1868. Tsune'emon's actions were a harbinger of what was to come.

A man of few wants, content to be able to eke out a living as a samurai, Tsune'emon sent as promised for his wife and child. The child, a boy named Sennosuke, had safely survived infancy. Tsune'emon's sister came too, so overnight Tsune'emon became head of a family, responsible for the well-being of four dependents: his wife, sister, Sennosuke, and later on his mother, who also joined them from Tottori.

This became Nobu's family. She thrived on the milk of her wet-nurse. A healthy child, she was soon crawling. From her infancy, she showed remarkable muscular coordination. Soon it was summer, and at eight months, she was a roly-poly baby. One in four children then died before their first birthday, and in a city like Kyoto where epidemics raged, only half of all children reached adulthood. Having lost four of his five offspring, Tsune'emon had been apprehensive about Nobu's chances, but now, confident that she would survive, he wrote a letter to the young lord in Iga Ueno to tell him the good news.

Soon after, Tsune'emon received an unexpected summons from the head priest of Chion'in. Seated in the main hall were Koyama, Iwanami, Takeda, and other temple dignitaries. As Tsune'emon sat humbly before them, a piece of paper was ceremoniously read aloud—and from that moment on he was, at long last, a true samurai. The young lord had clearly put in a good word for him. Now Tsune'emon and his descendants were entitled in perpetuity to the administrative position of *terazamurai* at Chion'in Temple.

Chion'in was in a sense unique, a temple so closely tied to the shogunate that it was viewed as a local branch office of the Tokugawa government. The Tokugawa name achieved nationwide fame thanks in large part to Chion'in. The clan founder was an intinerant monk named Tokuami, surnamed Matsudaira, who spread Pure Land teachings. His grandson invited the chief priest of Chion'in to the remote countryside of Mikawa (present-day Aichi Prefecture) to establish a family temple called Daijūji. "Great Tree Temple." As Great Tree was also a respectful term for the shogun, clearly the Matsudaira had grand ambitions. Establishing the temple catapulted the family to fame as protectors of Chion'in, the Grand Head Temple of the Pure Land Sect. Zongyū, the son of Matsudaira Chikatada (1431–1501), the fourth head of the family, became the twenty-fifth head of Chion'in by command of Emperor Gokashiwabara (1464–1526). Zongyū was the first in the Matsudaira line to become nationally known, eighty years before the rise to supreme power of Tokugawa Ieyasu (1543–1616), who was born Matsudaira Takechiyo.

When Ieyasu took power, he lost no time in refurbishing Chion'in and making it the Tokugawa headquarters in Kyoto. Head priests were chosen from imperial princes and treated as adopted sons of the shogun, traveling often to Edo and back. Kyoto children, seeing the enormous size of the Chion'in gate, said, "Tokugawa-san watches the emperor from the top of that gate. If anything's wrong, he flies a flag to signal Nijō Castle." The well at Chion'in was connected to the castle, according to an unfounded rumor that many people believed. Yet it is true that Tokugawa ninja set up camp in that district. Moreover, the grave of Yamaoka Dōami, who led Ieyasu to victory at Sekigahara by rounding up Kōga School ninja, is located in the Chion'in compound.

Chion'in also had intimate ties to the Tōdō family, who from the days of Takatora had been granted the fief of Iga, birthplace of the Iga School of ninjutsu, and served the Tokugawa faithfully by keeping an eye on the western daimyo. This domain played a key role in maintaining Tokugawa dominance over the western domains. Few outside daimyo—those labeled as enemies for having fought on the wrong side at Sekigahara—were as useful to the Tokugawa as the Tōdō. It is possible that someone in the Tōdō family put in a word for Tsune'emon. In any case, he acquired a hereditary post at Chion'in.

"The young lord said he would look out for me," mused Tsune'emon, cradling Nobu in his arms, "and this must be what he meant. I believe I owe my good fortune to this child." He felt rewarded for the responsibility he had assumed. His son was eight. He and his wife lavished affection on Nobu; she was lucky to be raised by this warmhearted couple.

As Nobu grew, she amazed the grownups around her. Not only was she a strikingly beautiful child, but whatever she did, she excelled in. When they put a writing-brush in her hand just to see what would happen, she was soon writing skillfully and begging them to teach her new characters. At five she could write complete sentences, and at six she penned a poem any adult would be proud to have written.

The section of town where they lived—Fukuro-machi, Chion'in Monzen—happened to be home to a number of writers and artists. Ike no Taiga (1723–1776), the celebrated master of poetry, calligraphy, and painting, had lived there until recently, and around this time, across the street from the Confucian scholar Murase Kōtei (1746–1818), someone new moved in: an odd old man named Ueda Akinari (1734–1809). His fingers were stiff and malformed but he used them dexterously and was always writing something. The grownups found him crotchety, but he was kind to children and, if they stared, would make his lame hands move like crabs. After he found out that little Nobu wrote *waka* poetry, this literary genius, author of the ghost-story collection *Tales of Moonlight and Rain*, gave her warm smiles and willingly corrected her works. She received an ideal form of special education for the gifted. Her poems showed swift improvement.

If that were all, Nobu would have merely been another beautiful and talented little girl, but surprisingly, she grew keen on fencing. When Sennosuke started his lessons she tagged along, though eight years his junior, and watched. At home when he practiced with a wooden sword, she imitated him, brandishing a stick. She remained in her adoptive parents' eyes a precious princess whose keeping they were responsible for, and so, for fear that her face might be scarred, they put a stop to it. "Goodness, how dangerous!" her mother exclaimed. "Girl shouldn't do such things." But Nobu didn't want to stop. At practice sessions she looked on with such tearful longing that Tsune'emon relented: "Well, all right then, just a little." At that, she beamed, picked up her wooden sword, and wouldn't let go. From then on, whenever he oversaw Sennosuke's practice, she would be right there, waving her sword and shouting *"Ei! Ei!"* in her sweet childish voice.

Around this time Nobu must have become aware that she was adopted. Her wet-nurse Takahashi continued to care for her even after she was weaned, dropping hints about her origins. That may help to explain why the girl was so eager to learn her brother's lessons. She did her best to keep up, as if trying to heal some sort of psychic wound. Tsune'emon seemed to sense this, and he taught her everything he taught her brother, without prejudice.

At fifteen, Sennosuke came of age and went through the *gempuku* ritual, a ceremonial cutting of the forelock. He was of delicate build, and people said behind his back that his little sister was stronger than him "even without the sword."

She would have been around seven when a strange samurai came calling. The unusual visitor brought a message from her real father in Iga Ueno: "What is Nobu doing now? I want to see her." Told this, Nobu froze, fearing she would be taken away from her loving home. Nothing could have been more terrifying to the little girl. "I'm ashamed of who I am," she said and hid herself, according to the later recollection of her wet-nurse's child. As a result, all talk of a meeting between her and her real father was laid aside.

A short while later came notice of a death: "On August 2, Lord Tōdō Shinshichirō passed away." Her real father's brief life had ended at age thirty-two. Nobu felt great remorse. "He must have sent the messenger because he was sick and wanted to see me once before he died. Yet I turned him away. What cruelty!" Her regret must have remained an open wound. Even later in life, as Rengetsu, she never spoke of it.

Nobu underwent a change. Her innocent features now bore a shadow of care. The records give no indication of any conversation she may have had with Tsune'emon this year, so nothing certain can be said, but it is possible to make an intelligent guess. She must have spoken with him about her mother, who was presumably still alive. Nobu was a spirited, strong-minded girl. Having lost her natural father, she might well have asked where her birth mother was and what she was doing. She might even have come right out and asked to meet her.

Inevitably, her father's death brought significant changes in the girl's life. Had he remained alive, she could one day have married into a suitable samurai family. Given her looks, intelligence, and talent, she might easily have had plenty of marriage offers, even from house elders or direct shogunal vassals. Tsune'emon had harboured hopes along those lines. His dearest wish was for her to develop her abilities to the full and find happiness. However, the death of her real father effectively closed off the path to a distinguished marriage.

That same year, Tsune'emon was finally allowed to surrender the surname Yamazaki, which he had taken to gain the post at Chion'in, and call himself Ōtagaki. He gave up the name Tsune'emon as well, becoming Ōtagaki Banzaemon Teruhisa. Sennosuke also changed his name, becoming Ōtagaki Mataichi Katahisa. Father and son served together at Chion'in from then on. Fifteen years after leaving Tottori, Tsune'emon—or Teruhisa, as we shall now call him—had at last achieved the goal he set for himself, that of raising the Ōtagaki family to the samurai class. But Nobu's future continued to weigh on his mind.

Until then, Teruhisa had been motivated solely by pity for the girl, but now he began to give serious thought to her future. The immediate question was whether it was appropriate for her to continue to live under the same roof as his son. The problem was, she was just too good-looking. Though they had grown up as brother and sister, they were not blood relations. Now that she no longer had the backing of her father, one possibility was for them to marry; otherwise, to protect her from ugly rumors she would have to leave the house. She was maturing quickly and already showing signs of womanly grace.

Teruhisa no doubt felt that Nobu's gifts shouldn't go to waste. With proper molding, she might become a light of the nation—but not if she stayed in the home of a poor temple samurai like him. The best course, he decided, would be to put her into service as lady-in-waiting at a daimyo's castle and let her be educated on a wider stage.

He summoned Nobu, sat her down in front of him, and told her earnestly that her real mother was married and living in nearby Kameyama. He urged her to go into service with the lord of Kameyama, pointing out that she could polish her accomplishments and take new lessons, too. As he spoke, his wife, who had raised Nobu from babyhood, sat by and listened, red-eyed.

Nobu faced her future squarely. Armed with dual hope, having heard that her mother was alive and that she would be able to take lessons in all sorts of new things, she went willingly to Kameyama Castle. Whatever may have passed between Nobu and her mother—if indeed they ever met—is unknown. Rengetsu never said a word on the subject.

In Kameyama, she applied herself to her lessons with fierce intensity. In addition to poetry, she became so proficient in dancing, sewing, and other feminine accomplishments that she could teach others. As she turned ten, then fifteen, becoming ever more beautiful, she attracted notice. It was only a matter of time, people speculated, before the daimyo made her his mistress.

But soon those same people were shaking their heads: "She's impossible!" Too mannish, they meant. Her martial art skills were by now considerable. If she had stuck to the halberd, a weapon deemed acceptable for women, that would have been all right, but in her spare moments she still practiced fencing with a wooden sword. She managed to find someone to teach her the *kusarigama* (sickle and chain) and could soon wield it with deadly accuracy. She was always hanging around the stables, and before anyone quite knew it she was straddling a horse, learning to ride. The final touch was a bamboo pole. She got one somewhere and used it to practice vaulting over castle fences.

The other ladies-in-waiting were appalled that one of them should be so nearly a ninja. "Her beauty may have won her admirers," they sniffed, "but her actions are a disgrace."

Late in life, after retiring near Kamigamo Shrine in Kyoto, Rengetsu would declare, "Old lady that I am, if I had a three-foot pole, I could still vault a six-foot fence."

Despite these shocking ways, when you saw her sit composing an elegant poem or doing nothing at all, she looked more demure and graceful than anyone.

Once when she came home to Kyoto for a holiday, an ugly incident took place. She went to Kiyomizu Temple with some friends to admire the fall leaves, and what should they see but four or five drunken louts come walking toward them. Nobu tensed, sensing trouble. Then one of the louts stretched out his arms on either side, barring the way, and the others moved in. The girls shrieked and tried to escape. "Please leave us alone. Let us go by," Nobu pleaded. The men only grew bolder and grabbed the girls. One of them buried his nose in the back of Nobu's neck, smelling her skin, and groped her breast through the front of her kimono. In that moment all her training paid off. She grabbed him by the scruff of his neck, picked him up, and threw him on the ground. When the others saw that, they stopped what they were doing, exchanged glances, and scattered like baby spiders. The girls, unable to immediately digest what had happened, merely stood saucer-eyed.

The Collected Works of the Nun Rengetsu contains the comment, "Great beauty though she was, Nobu was also a woman of ability."

This incident caused a stir in the neighborhood. Teruhisa was astonished. He had hoped that sending Nobu to the castle would make her more modest and ladylike, but instead she had attained a certificate of mastery of the halberd, could execute a judo throw against a male opponent, knew how to use a sickle and chain, and could vault a six-foot fence.

She was different from other girls in other ways, too.

Wanting her to wear kimono like an ordinary girl, Teruhisa had her go out dressed in a brightly-colored long-sleeved kimono. And then one day another incident took place.

Nobu paused in front of an antique store to admire a large ceramic figure of Daruma on display. It was a charming piece, a gem. She decided she wanted her father to see it and asked the price, which was reasonable, so she bought it on the spot. The dealer offered to deliver the piece, but Nobu brushed his offer aside. She couldn't wait to take it home and show her father, and besides, she knew her arms were strong enough to carry it. So off she strode through town, a lovely young lady of seventeen dressed in a gorgeous long-sleeved kimono and lugging a big figure of Daruma under her arm. Naturally she attracted eyes and catcalls. Men passing by tugged on one another's sleeves and pointed. Some called out, "What're you doing, dearie?" She was overcome with embarrassment, her cheeks scarlet. Such a crowd of men started trailing behind her that she ran into a roadside house for refuge. Unfortunately, no one was home. Unable to entreat whoever lived there to keep the Daruma for her temporarily, she simply left it there and fled. This provoked more jesting. Nobu was the opposite of a thief, people laughed. "Who else would break into your house, just to leave something there?"

Others might laugh, but for Teruhisa, anxious to marry Nobu into a good family, such behavior was too visible. He decided the best course might be simply to keep her at home. Recent changes in the household left him little choice. First Katahisa died at the age of twenty. Then, heartbroken at the death of her only son, his wife wasted away until, less than three months later, she too was gone. Without an heir, the Ōtagaki family would perish. About other things Teruhisa was indifferent, but where preserving the family name was concerned he was almost comically obsessed. He began to search for a young man to adopt, perhaps seeking in this way to assuage his grief.

He circulated a notice declaring his intent to adopt a son "suited to the Ōtagaki family" and, through his connections, fetched from the town of Kinosaki in far-off Tajima Province a youth named Tainoshō Tenzō. This was the fourth son of the village headman, a respected local man and a distant kinsman. Teruhisa renamed him Ōtagaki Mochihisa and brought him home. Around the house he was known as Naoichi.

When Nobu came home from the castle on leave she would see Naoichi, but there was something dark and lonely about him. To cheer him up she tried her best to draw him out, but his eyes never brightened; he would make some hollow reply, and the conversation would lag. Teruhisa told her to address Naoichi as "elder brother," but she felt uncomfortable doing so. She couldn't help remembering the half-brother who had been so frail and yet so intelligent and kind. Deep down Teruhisa seemed to feel the same way, and struggled to accept this youth who was so much less gifted than his flesh-and-blood son had been.

Naoichi seemed to sense how they felt about him. As if resigned to living under a gray cloud for the rest of his life, he wore a glum expression and lolled about. Nobu was sympathetic since she too was adopted, but somehow the two of them never became close. For three years, every time she came home on leave from the castle she spent days in his company, yet there was no deep connection between them.

The passage of time brought the inevitable physical changes to them both. Nobu was no longer a girl but a young woman. Naoichi's voice changed, and each time she came home she found him noticeably more masculine. The change repelled rather than attracted her—and then her grandmother died, leaving no woman to help around the house. This time Nobu came home for good. Teruhisa urged her to marry Naoichi, whom she had known for years without a whiff of romance. She felt sorry for her widowed father and sympathized with Naoichi, who had been torn from his real family. In the end, despite her lack of interest, she agreed to the marriage.

And so Nobu was wed. People talked long afterward of her beauty at the age of seventeen as, dressed in bridal finery, she sat at her nuptials, the crowning happiness of a woman's life. Inside she was a morass of wordless emotions. She felt no joy, had no expectation of happiness. Anxiety welled up in her heart. The marriage showed no promise of leading to mature love.

When she was seventy, Rengetsu mentioned Naoichi in a letter. All she said was, "Since we were childhood friends, I would like to visit Naoichi's grave." She didn't refer to him as her husband. In her mind, he remained a "childhood friend."

Teruhisa, however, didn't understand how she felt. At the wedding, with the young couple seated side by side, he was in high spirits. "Our two families, the Ōtagaki and the Tainoshō, are both descended from Prince Onome. We are, in a manner of speaking, fraternally related. Long ago when we belonged to the Yamana clan, we aided one another as allies. I am delighted to have an adopted son of pure blood."

Genealogy did indicate that the Ōtagaki family could trace its ancestry to Prince Onome. At Onome Shrine the family had long worshipped him as its tutelary deity. But since the prince had lived over a millennium ago, back in the ancient Kofun period (250–538), the two families were as good as unrelated. Nevertheless Teruhisa, obsessed with family lineage, saw this as a distinguished bloodline. He not only sought out the "pedigreed" youth in the wilds of Tajima and dragged him to the capital but also married him to Nobu. His actions were earnest but preposterous. Nobu was forced to marry someone she didn't even like, for the absurd reason that he was descended from Prince Onome. Still, she was relieved to see her father happy again, freed from the gloom that had enveloped him since losing his wife. As an orphan, she knew only too well the loneliness of losing family. She chose to accept her fate and bear it patiently.

And yet the fate awaiting her was cruel; her life with Naoichi was hellish. Some doubt this, but it must be so. Historian Murakami Sodō gathered information on Rengetsu's life, unearthing details on how wretched her married life was by tracking down the child of her wet-nurse Takahashi and consulting with people in Naoichi's hometown. He found that Naoichi ignored both the family business and his young wife; got into bad company and became a licentious loafer as well as a compulsive gambler and drinker; and finally quarreled with his adopted father and physically abused Nobu. This account must be near the truth.

At first, the marriage seemed amicable enough. Naoichi stayed home, and soon a son was born to them. The couple's joy didn't last. The baby fed poorly and may have caught some infectious disease, rapidly losing strength and dying before he was a month old. Nobu buried the tiny remains in Chion'in cemetery. The death of his son may have been Naoichi's undoing. He began staying out more and more. Nobu took this as a sign of male weakness, but if she reproached him, he would be even less inclined to come home. Weak from childbirth, despondent from the loss of her firstborn, and betrayed by her husband, she bore her plight with patience—but doing so only worked against her. He felt she was mocking him, and ended by striking her.

From the first, Naoichi had never done well at anything. His mother's hopes were pinned on his elder brother, who was smarter and more likable. Naoichi was convinced that that was why he'd been put up for adoption to this family in the capital, so far from home. This sense of being abandoned doubtless accounted for the listless look in his eyes. Moreover, his wife and fellow adoptee was well known in the capital for her beauty and accomplishments. She came from the prestigious Tōdō family, too, so even in his pedigree he couldn't compete. Nobu's heart ached all the more because she understood the reasons behind her husband's bad behavior.

Perhaps if there were another child, he would settle down. Clinging to this faint hope, Nobu submitted to his embraces, but the result never varied. At twenty she gave birth to a girl who died at age two, just at her sweetest. At twenty-two she had another girl who died when she was four. One after another, all her children died. With each death, Naoichi grew more dissipated.

There was no letup in sad news, as next her husband's mother died. Hearing that her mother-in-law was dying, she went to Osaka, where Naoichi's brother practiced medicine, only to find the old woman lying cold and dead inside a mosquito net. The shadows in Naoichi's eyes grew deeper. He became lethargic, barely even taking meals, until finally he was so weak that he couldn't perform his duties in the temple.

At long last Teruhisa realized his folly in setting such store by the ancient genealogy and bringing Naoichi back with him. He resigned himself to the inevitability of divorce, but Nobu demurred. "Wait another year and a half," she said. "I'll talk to him." She feared for Naoichi—if she divorced him, severing the slender thread that bound them and leaving him to drift alone in the world, what might become of him? She felt an unpleasant presentiment.

"His brother is a physician, isn't he?" said Teruhisa. "Maybe he should go stay with him to recuperate. Anyway, he can't stay here."

Nobu wept. It was true that her husband was dissipated. But should she cast him to the winds? Did she have the strength to care for him from now on? Everyone urged her to end the marriage, adding, "With your looks, you'd have all kinds of good offers." Such comments only brought new tears. The man she had grown up with and married was suffering from what deserved to be called an illness. Leaving him and, if fortunate enough to find a good match, remarrying would only increase his forlornness. That thought held her back. It wasn't that she was trying to be a good wife but that she didn't have the heart to be inhumane.

And yet there was the family's responsibility to Chion'in to consider. Ōtagaki men were bound to serve the temple. If Naoichi could not carry out his duties, he must go. Reluctantly Nobu consented to a divorce, yielding to her father's wishes on one condition—that she need never marry again.

And so Nobu and Naoichi parted ways. He went to stay with his brother in Osaka, but the divorce effectively killed him. He died not long afterward, a broken man.

Word of his passing came just as cool autumn breezes were beginning to blow. Nobu couldn't face the harvest moon, which was said to reflect people's hearts. Long afterward she continued to blame herself for the horror brought about by the darkness in her heart. Half a century later, after she had become the nun Rengetsu, she wrote a letter to Naoichi's brother ending with this reflective, almost confessional poem:

> Afraid lest
> The moon may ask about
> Things long past,
> Tonight I find my eyes
> Turning ever downward.

Poetry was a solace to her. Now twenty-five and living alone with her adoptive father, she once again took up its study. Her neighborhood was filled with men of learning, and of them all she was drawn most to Ueda Akinari, the one who had taught her when she was small. She'd been too young then to genuinely apply herself; the lessons had been a form of play. But now the great writer, known for his obstinacy, would take no pupils. He was known for kicking intruders out, and rarely allowed visitors. When applicants came to his door he would wave his cane or even beat them with it to make them go away.

By this time Akinari was in his late seventies and blind. He dragged himself around with difficulty, and his lifestyle was decidedly eccentric, but his eccentricities appealed to her. Besides brushes and inkstones he had only a few tea utensils and an old futon in his house. On losing his wife of many years, to her astonishment he rolled around on the tatami mats, stamped his feet, and cried like a baby. His adopted daughter, a nun, came to take care of him, but eventually he moved close to Nanzenji Temple, bought a small tea field, and lived out his remaining days brewing and sipping tea.

This strange old man taught Nobu several important things about poetry. A poet named Kagawa Kageki (1768–1843) was beginning to take Kyoto by storm. Also known by the name Keien, like her adoptive father he was from Tottori, so Nobu couldn't help noticing him. Yet Ueda Akinari flatly said his poetry rang hollow. "His poetry contains no truth, and only sings." In other words, Kagawa emphasized euphony without conveying deep emotions. At the same time, Akinari never failed to hold up the late Ozawa Roan as a positive example. "He was my heart's true companion. If you want to learn about poetry, learn from him."

Ozawa Roan (1723–1801) had been another eccentric. He was by nature incapable of tolerating dishonesty or deviousness in others, and he never used flattery. Once a friend sent him some prawns. Where most people would write a letter of thanks, Roan wrote, "I cannot tell a lie. I didn't want to be sick to my stomach, so I didn't eat any." When someone sent him some Shinshū buckwheat noodles he wrote, "The batch I received before had no impurities in the flour, but these did." Largely because of this inability to accommodate himself to social expectations, he remained poor his whole life. At one time he had been a vassal of the Takatsukasa clan, but when ordered to leave his aged mother and travel to Kantō, he moaned so incessantly about her on the road that finally he was dismissed and became a masterless samurai. After that he made his living through poetry. He also often came to see Ueda Akinari and poke his nose in the master's business, Nobu heard.

Motoori Norinaga (1730–1801), the eminent scholar of Shinto and Japanese classics, called Roan "the greatest poet of this generation." Members of the Mitsui family (the later zaibatsu), hearing of his fame, all studied with him. They paid him handsomely, but he expelled the lot of them because once when he lay ill in bed, none of them came to see him. Only his impoverished students came calling. Roan, who took such matters seriously, decided that wealthy magnates lacked human feeling. He sent the family this poem:

> Wealth in this world
> Is but the light in a drop of dew
> Upon a blade of grass
> Gleaming while it awaits
> The coming breeze.

In other words, "Life is short. Wealth is nothing but a glimmer of light that vanishes when you die. People who have no inkling of what is most important in life aren't fit to study poetry." To Roan this made perfect sense, but in the eyes of the world it made him an oddball. In any case, he despised superficial relationships. Better than anyone in his age, he revealed the poverty of living in thrall to something that made you untrue to yourself.

In the course of hearing such anecdotes, Nobu became interested in Roan. She obtained a collection of his poetry and read it till it nearly fell apart. His poems were direct and piercing. They could not have been more different from the hidebound, conservative style of Kagawa Kageki. Roan preached the importance of writing *tadagoto-uta*—poems that describe something directly without resorting to metaphor or simile. He believed that poetry consists in expressing thoughts of the moment at hand, in words of one's own that have the ring of truth. Furthermore, he believed that poetry was "a path to making one's heart honest."

Nobu was particularly drawn by this idea. Why, she had always wondered, did people lose their way and become unhappy? Poetry to her was a kind of guidepost to use in pondering such matters, and Roan's poetry seemed to offer an answer to her deepest questions. She began copying out his poems.

> Choosing not
> The wide, smooth road
> People of this world
> Tread the rocky path of guile
> And so they lose their way.

While writing out Roan's poem, Nobu thought about her own guile. From the time she was little, people had praised her abilities. She had mastered every art or skill she ever set out to acquire. Her physical appearance had won praise as well. Over time she had learned to adapt in order to gain acceptance, submitting first to her father and then to her husband. She had chosen the way of a dutiful wife, and yet perhaps in doing so she had brought unhappiness to Naoichi and others. When talk of marriage came up, why hadn't she spoken up and said she didn't want to marry him? Even after the wedding, perhaps if she had let herself cry when she wanted to or get angry with him when she felt like it, he might still be alive. But she hadn't done that. She had worn a face like a Noh mask and played the part of a wise wife. And for all she knew, she had driven her husband to his death. These thoughts haunted her.

> Honest, simple words
> And an honest, simple heart

Are the sign of one
Who is set upon the path
To ancient virtue.

Poetry was the way to live with a true and honest heart, Roan wrote. These words of his struck home to her. Words, however many one might write, lacked substance if one focused only on their beauty. Words were the cry of the heart, so they had to convey the whole, the substance, of what one felt. Human thoughts craved utterance, in the same way that trees and grasses lent their voices to the wind…

Encouraged by Roan's poetry and example, Nobu began to express her thoughts in *waka*.

Talk of her remarrying came up in the spring of the fourth year after the collapse of her first marriage. Actually, even before that her father had received frequent inquiries from would-be suitors. By this time twenty-nine, she looked as young and lovely as ever. No one would have taken her for a day over twenty. True, she was thinner, but this only gave her a willowy grace that enhanced her beauty all the more. When she walked about in Kyoto, men's glances followed her. She scurried to her destination in order to avoid those glances, a habit unchanged from childhood.

For three years, out of respect for her feelings her father had refrained from broaching the topic of remarriage, but he was now sixty-five and much frailer than before. Carrying out his duties at the temple had become a burdensome task. Sometimes he would indulge in useless regrets, lamenting the death of his son Katahisa and wishing helplessly that Katahisa and Nobu could have lived with him as man and wife. Now and again she would find him kneeling before the Buddhist altar, staring at his dead son's memorial tablet.

All of this was exceedingly painful to Nobu. Teruhisa, her adoptive father, was her only living relative. The last thing she wanted to do was cause him pain and loneliness. Watching him lose all vitality and grow ever more hollow-eyed, all because she wouldn't consider marrying again, tore at her heart.

Normally, samurai retired at age sixty. Some asked to retire even earlier, at around fifty. For Teruhisa to keep on performing his duties at sixty-five, still with no successor on the horizon, was highly unusual. In deference to her he had steadily declined all offers from those interested in becoming his adopted son-in-law. Because of her, he dragged his aged body to work every day.

If I just am patient and endure what comes... As before, such thoughts began to go through Nobu's mind. She resolved to yield once more to her father's wishes. "Father," she told him briskly, "life is short. There's no telling when something may happen even to you. After thinking it through, I've come to the conclusion that I have no choice but to marry again."

To Teruhisa these were welcome words indeed, beyond what he had hoped. But he knew what was in her heart. "Nobu, are you sure? I was born a farmer in Tottori, and this temple gave me a hereditary post as samurai. I owe it to the temple not to let my family die out. I have to adopt a successor, but there is another way to do it. I could leave you alone and adopt a pair of strangers, husband and wife, to take the Ōtagaki name and carry on after me."

Nobu was silent. "Let me make a selfish request," he continued. "You may not be of my blood, but you're still my only daughter, and I'm proud of you. From the time I first adopted you I've been thrilled to be your father. Every time someone praised you, I felt as happy as if the praise were meant for me—no, happier! I shouldn't say or think such things, but to tell the truth, when your real father died, deep down I was relieved. I knew then I'd never have to give you up. You were completely mine. Let me be honest. I want more than anything in this world to have a child of yours become head of the Ōtagaki family."

Tears fell from his eyes. Never before had Nobu seen her father weep. She too misted over. For the first time since her adoption, she felt that she had gained a true place in the world.

"All right," she said. "I'll take a husband to carry on the Ōtagaki name. But Father, I have a longstanding wish, and that is to become a nun and serve Buddha. If my next husband should die, that very day I would like to shave my head. Will you allow me to do that?"

"Of course. This is the last request I will ever make of you. If such a dreadful thing should happen, I too will renounce the world and become a priest."

Determined never to subject his daughter to misery again, Teruhisa exercised utmost care in choosing a new husband for her. The man he settled on was Ishikawa Jūjirō, the third son of Ishikawa Kōji Mitsusada, a vassal of Ii Kamon-no-kami, the daimyo of Hikone. What followed was perhaps the happiest time of Nobu's life.

Jūjirō turned out to be every bit as kindly as her father had hoped. The house of Ii in Hikone was known for the fierceness of its warriors, who had earned the nickname "Red Devils" at the battle of Sekigahara. Those days were long gone, however, and Jūjirō bore not a trace of that legendary roughness. Rather, he was delicate of build, a graceful young man with a gentle, benevolent smile, modest in all things but never subservient. Teruhisa and he would set out for work at Chion'in every day like father and son, carrying their lunches tied at the waist.

People were glad that Nobu had married such a good man. For the first time, she experienced the joys of married life. She soon gave birth to a little girl, and her father could not have been more delighted. "I have no regrets in life," he said, and went into retirement, letting Jūjirō take his place as head of the family. And then the longed-for male heir was born.

And yet Nobu continued to be dogged by misfortune. One chilly spring day in her fourth year of marriage, she and Jūjirō went on a family outing to see the cherry blossoms in Higashiyama. From that day on, he had a bad cough. At first she thought little of it, assuming he had merely caught a cold, but although he saw a doctor and took medicine, his condition didn't improve. He had a low-grade fever and finally took to his bed. Nobu never left his side. Despite the midsummer heat, she never so much as undid her obi, but cared for him morning and night. Even so, he continued to weaken. By the time of the May rains he was so emaciated he had passed the point of no return, and by the end of June he lay near death.

Nobu made up her mind to renounce the world while her husband was still conscious. Kneeling before him, she began to cut off her glossy black hair. She wanted him to know before he died that she would devote the rest of her life to praying for his soul.

The next day Jūjirō died. Nobu, now thirty-three, was a widow for the second time.

For the next few months, she was in a wretched state, as everyone could see. A letter that she wrote shortly after losing her husband has survived in the Ono family of Kaiya-machi: "Even as I open letters and gifts, all seems like a dream." For a while she was in a stupor. All day long she held her late husband's clothing and looked at the various articles he had given her.

Later she composed poems about her husband's cremation:

Smoke rises
Till the sky turns dark,
And I weep
Feeling as though the end
Will bring me no surcease.

Standing below
Higashiyama hills
Where together we saw
The cherry blossoms,
I feel only sadness.

In summer the thirty-six hills of the Higashiyama range were a vibrant green, and soon the midsummer Bon festival would arrive, when the hillsides were lit with bonfires to guide the spirits of the dead on their return to the netherworld; even then, her grief was unassuaged.

But grief and sadness could not occupy her forever. She had an infant son and a five-year-old daughter, and her father, now old, also needed her care. He decided that he would take the tonsure as well, and from the Ii family connected with Jūjirō he brought Tasaburō, the younger brother of Hikone retainer Kazami Heima, to become head of the Ōtagaki family. The adoption took place with the understanding that when Nobu's son became an adult, headship of the family would revert to him. In samurai families, a grandson could follow his grandfather as head of the family. If the grandson was too young to take up his duties, then someone was adopted into the family to manage in the interim. This sort of arrangement was common.

And so, having ensured that the Ōtagaki name would not die out, Teruhisa requested permission to enter the priesthood. In consideration of his store of knowledge concerning Chion'in he was made chief priest of the sub-temple Makuzuan, a great honor. The sub-temple was named after Makuzugahara, a picturesque valley to the south. In the past, it had been overgrown with pampas grass and a woody vine called *makuzu* (scarlet kadsura, *kadsura japonica*), and foxes had made their dens there. It was there that the monk-poet Saigyō (1118–1190) composed his iconic poem:

> Let me die
> Under the cherry blossoms
> In springtime
> Around the time of the full moon
> In the second lunar month.

With such rich literary significance, Makuzugahara might easily have become an *utamakura*, a place name used allusively in classical poetry. In the Muromachi period six retreats called the "Kyoto Rokuami" stood there, providing food and entertainment for those who enjoyed elegant pastimes, including Ashikaga shoguns. These were the first establishments to serve *kaiseki ryōri*, Japan's multi-course haute cuisine. Although small, Makuzuan was therefore well known to local literati. Motoori Norinaga, for one, came to compose extemporaneous prose and poetry—probably because this was where Saigyō had declared his wish to die under a full moon and cherries in full bloom. Taking the first character of Saigyō's name, the Chion'in chief priest gave Teruhisa the Buddhist name Saishin, "Saigyō's Mind," and to Nobu he gave the name Rengetsu, "Lotus Moon."

Father and daughter moved into Makuzuan together with the two small children. There may seem something peculiar about a nun with small children, but Chion'in was relaxed about such things. Indeed, many of the priests kept women in the compound, de facto wives known as *daikokuhan*. After the strait-laced Matsudaira Sadanobu (1759–1829) became senior councilor of the Tokugawa shogunate, that practice was banned for a time, causing an uproar, but the fuss soon ended and everything went back to the way it had been.

The entrance to Makuzuan is interesting. At Chion'in, if you enter through the main entrance, you must climb a steep hill. On the right is the so-called "female slope," with more easily negotiable stairs, and Makuzuan is halfway up that slope. Just within the gate is a small lotus pond with a stone bridge that visitors must cross.

Nobu—or rather Rengetsu—liked to stand on that bridge and look down on the lotus blossoms below. A single slender stalk would rise from the mud toward the heavens, and at its tip would be a lotus blossom of such exquisite beauty that it seemed unearthly, as if it might truly have come from the moon. How could a flower so beautiful rise out of muck?

Accompanied by her father and children, Rengetsu found life at Makuzuan fulfilling. For the first time in her thirty-three years, she felt at peace.

The moss garden was beautiful. Grandfather Saishin beamed to see the five-year-old at play with her toddler brother while he taught Rengetsu the game of go. The more she played the more proficient she became, and soon she was playing at the lowest professional level. Saishin joked that she might be able to make a living by teaching others. Soon his partners were requesting to play against her, but no matter how they begged, she would smilingly decline. After they gave up and left, her father would laugh. "They're more interested in staring at your face than at the go board!"

These halcyon days seemed likely to go on forever, but this was not the case. First the little girl died, shortly after her seventh birthday. On April 8, she sipped hydrangea tea in happy celebration of the Buddha's birthday, and then all of a sudden she was gone. Two years later, at New Year's, the little boy died, too. All Rengetsu's children were now dead, leaving only their little kimono as mementoes.

The loss of his grandchildren came as a dreadful blow to Saishin. Even though he had become a priest in hopes of severing his blind passions, once it became heartbreakingly clear to him that there was no hope of continuing the Ōtagaki line through his grandchildren, he aged rapidly. Every year at the midsummer Bon festival to honor the dead he would break off sprays of bush clover, one for each departed child and grandchild, and lay them on their graves. He did that for five years, and then on August 15, 1832, as bonfires blazed to see off the spirits of the dead, he quietly passed away, his life burnt out at the age of seventy-eight.

Rengetsu was bereft. Since Makuzuan wasn't a nunnery, she was unable to take over her father's position. At forty-two, she was still beautiful, with porcelain skin that men couldn't help noticing. When the new head priest came, it wouldn't do to have such a nun in the compound. She had nowhere to go. Forlornly she climbed the stairs behind the Main Hall of the Chion'in till she came to the Ōtagaki graves in the bleak cemetery. Dressed in black, she stood among the graves of all her dead, lingering even after the sun went down and the graveyard was pitch dark.

People pleaded with her to be reasonable. "It's too dangerous! What if someone rips your clothes off and rapes you?" Finally she came down from the cemetery, but day after day she would return and stay from dawn till dusk, brooding. She decided she wanted to live there. She said she would put up a tiny hut in the Ōtagaki corner, but this was of course nonsense. The temple talked her out of the idea, reminding her that cemeteries are not for the living. Later on she wrote, "I longed to be near my father's grave, but the mountaintop was no place for the living, so sadly I moved to Kagura Okazaki."

She rented a hut at the foot of a hill on the outskirts of Shōgoin village, amid rice paddies and fields. Now she needed a livelihood. The easiest solution was to become a teacher of go—but that would have meant playing against men, which she was unwilling to do. She thought it over and realized that there were six other arts or pastimes that she was qualified to teach: the halberd, the chain and sickle, fencing, dancing, poetry, and sewing. But few of those paths were suitable. Martial arts were out of the question; a nun certainly couldn't teach others how to handle a sword and take a human life. Dancing was also inappropriate; she couldn't very well get up and dance in her black habit. Sewing was no good, either; there were better teachers than she in town. The only remaining possibility was poetry, although teaching poetry didn't promise to be very lucrative. She decided to take pupils anyway, but this venture did not turn out well.

Despite all she had been through, and despite being a nun, Rengetsu still remained an alluring woman whose beauty stirred men's hearts. Men flocked to her door saying they wanted to study poetry with her, but that was only an excuse to sit and drink in her charms. A few were serious, but they were the exceptions. Married men with children would openly proposition the lovely widow-turned-nun. Though determined not to hate, she soon became fed up with the male sex. Buddha's teaching was *shikisoku zekū*: Matter is void. And yet if she didn't look the way she did, would all these men come by? It seemed to her that she attracted the emptiness of the world in droves—just the opposite of what she sought in Buddhism.

She got an idea: she would remove her eyebrows. Surely that would spoil her appearance. One by one, she plucked out the hairs, hoping that now she would look old and ugly. Each twinge of pain made her glad. But of course, merely removing the eyebrows couldn't alter her innate loveliness. In later years the classical scholar Kondō Yoshiki (1801–1880), who met with her around this time, recalled, "She was dressed in soiled, rough clothing and she had removed her eyebrows, but somehow that only emphasized the beauty of her face."

Nasty rumors without a grain of truth soon spread. What was worse, men took to barging in when no one was around. A visitor would start out on some innocent topic, but soon his eyes would take on a dark gleam. "Come on," he would whisper. "You'll let me, won't you? You know you're lonely." Overcome by a disgust bordering on fear, she would shove him away and rush out the door. The disgust she felt only proved to her the shallowness of her spiritual training. It discouraged her yet more to think that she still had a woman's body. These torments were worse than being groped. As the product of an illicit union herself, moreover, she knew firsthand what sorrow could come of passion.

Men who came at her with barefaced lust were easier to deal with than one young man who wrote her heartfelt love letters. He begged her to renounce her vows and return to lay life: "If you marry me, I swear I will make you happy." There seemed no escaping such sincerity.

Finally she was driven to drastic action. "I have sworn to devote my life to serving Buddha," she told him. "Having you make these advances shows that I must strengthen my resolve. My appearance is the trouble. Wait here." With that she disappeared behind the *fusuma* sliding door. Moments later he heard a low moaning. He pushed open the door and there stood Rengetsu, spitting blood and waving her hands like a ghoul. Behind her was a pair of heavy scales connected by a blood-soaked thread to her mouth. At first he couldn't make out what the grisly scene meant, but then in a flash it was clear: she was standing with her fingers in her bloodied mouth, a string tied around her front teeth. To his horror, she was trying to make herself into a toothless hag. Already one bloodied tooth lay on the floor. In terrible pain, she was trying to pull out the rest. Every time she extracted a tooth, more blood poured from her mouth.

The man screamed. Half hysterical, he begged her: "Stop! Stop it!"

But Rengetsu went right on disfiguring herself. Groaning, she pulled out tooth after tooth. The sight was too much for the young man's nerves, and he fled outside.

After her teeth were gone, men finally left her alone. The earnest young man never returned. The nasty rumors ended. Villagers marveled, "She's stronger than any man. By some mistake she was born a woman. Come to think of it, she has a man's build, square shoulders and all." In this way Rengetsu finally obtained peace and quiet.

This is the story that's been handed down, though in Rengetsu's later years, after she became old and placid, people doubted its truth. The Confucian scholar Morita Sessai (1811–1868), teacher of the brilliant political thinker Yoshida Shōin (1830–1859), was an early skeptic. Once he asked Tomioka Tessai pointblank: "That story is fiction, isn't it?" But Tessai, who had grown up alongside Rengetsu, shook his head. "No, that's exactly the sort of thing she would have done."

No longer able to teach poetry, Rengetsu was once again at her wits' end.

With a dwindling store of rice, she began to lose weight. Now sunken-cheeked, she seemed on her way to becoming one of the hungry ghosts of Buddhist lore. Having no other choice, she took to *takuhatsu*, the Buddhist practice of begging for food and alms. She walked all the way to a place called Awataguchi, where an old woman she knew made her living producing a kind of pottery called Awata-yaki. The old woman catered to travelers. Her shop was on the edge of town, and travelers would stop to buy souvenirs before climbing

Keage Hill, heading east.

On seeing Rengetsu's emaciation, the old woman took pity on her and delicately suggested that she try her hand at pottery. "I know you write poetry. If you made pottery by hand and engraved poems on your works, you could easily make enough to live on. In winter your hands will get chilblains, so the work won't be easy, but it's interesting. I'll give you some clay and show you how to knead it. Why not give it a try?"

"It will ruin my hands?" Rengetsu's eyes gleamed with anticipation. Nothing could have suited her more.

Slender, graceful fingers were a symbol of feminine beauty. Anyone familiar with Kabuki will know that in the Edo period a woman's lithe, fingers were considered as alluring as a beautiful face. Partly that was because the kimono concealed the lines of the body, leaving only the hands exposed. Not until the twentieth century, when Western-style clothing became commonplace, did a woman's figure become a standard measure of beauty. And so it was that in Rengetsu's day, a woman with work-roughened hands and fingers was considered to have lost her looks.

Rengetsu devoted herself to pottery-making with a vengeance, hoping meanwhile that her physical appearance would change. Passionate by nature, she was determined to pursue this new occupation wherever it took her. In rain and wind, she walked to the old woman's place and learned from her the fundamentals of pottery. Presently she took clay home with her and worked it there, forgetting even to eat and sleep as she struggled to make it conform to her will. Her fingers became as rough and worn as those of an old woman, but that no longer mattered. The emergence from unclean clay of a beautiful vessel came to seem a form of salvation for her. Above all, she became convinced that there was virtue in ceramics. Clay, a thing of no intrinsic value, allowed everyone— young and old, male and female—to find work and make a living. No other occupation was like it.

She made small teapots known in the regional dialect as *kibisho*—a corruption of the Chinese-style pronunciation *kyūsha* from the Tang and Song dynasties. The countryside was filled with what were known as "instant *bunjin*" or men of letters. The reason was simple: from around the second half of the eighteenth century, wealth shifted from the samurai class to the people, and wealthy farmers and merchants around the country awoke to the pleasures of learning. Even farmers of modest means dabbled in Chinese literature and enjoyed Chinese-style decoration. Everyone aspired to the Chinese ideal of the *wenjin*, a scholar who was also practiced in the arts. Participating in the *sencha* tea ceremony was de rigueur. Kindred minds from neighboring regions would gather for tea and discussion before a Chinese-style scroll painting in the alcove. Such occasions required teapots, which people referred to by the Chinese-inspired name.

Rengetsu's *kibisho* were by no means artistically made. She was skilled in most other arts she turned her hand to, but in pottery she made little or no progress.

She would make a batch of fifty or a hundred teapots and teacups and, using a nail, incise them with poems of her own. Once a month she carted them from Awataguchi to a kiln on Kiyomizu-zaka Street that charged one silver coin to fire fifty, two to fire a hundred. Her works remained stubbornly amateurish. To fire them she sought the help of celebrated local ceramicists such as Taizan Yohei and Kiyomizu Rokubei, but her pieces weren't placed in the prized place in the center of the kiln. Shoved to the back, where the distribution of heat was uneven at best, they did not turn out well. Her wares were so rudimentary that she had trouble finding shops willing to carry them. The sight of her rough-and-ready works made shopkeepers frown. "They won't sell," they warned, and indeed sales lagged.

After visiting shop after shop that sold Kyoto souvenirs, she finally found one willing to stock her *kibisho*. She knew their imperfections better than anyone, but she had no other means of supporting herself. This poem expresses her dissatisfaction with her wares:

Taking the clumsy,
Fragile things I make
To sell them
In the marketplace—
How forlorn am I!

Shopkeepers spoke ill of her behind her back. To her face they were polite, but the moment she disappeared they criticized her in the crudest of terms, spreading unfounded rumors. One shopkeeper on Kiyomizu-zaka Street was especially bad. If a customer asked, "Whose work is this?" he would say, "That's by a nun named Rengetsu. Used to be a prostitute in Gion. Gorgeous. They say she's so oversexed, even after becoming a nun she'll drag a man into her bed." He and others sold Rengetsu's works while telling coarse, made-up stories about her. Perhaps customers found something appealing in such promotion; in any case, sales picked up.

The stories naturally came to Rengetsu's ears, too. So few shops were willing to stock her works to begin with that she had no choice but to keep on doing business with these dirty-minded men. Then she began to suspect that the reason such trifles bothered her lay in her own self-absorption. She was a small, insignificant being. If she cast aside all desire for fame and glory, then such trivial lies would no longer cause her suffering. She herself was far from pure in body or spirit, so what gave her the right to be indignant? In a pure world, she would have no place. She needed to absorb the discipline of *parātmasamatā*, "equality of self and others." She came to see the struggle to eliminate all distinction between herself and others as her lifelong task. From this time onward, her letters frequently contain the line, "I want to practice the equality of self and others."

That insight brought about a change in Rengetsu's artistic style. She began to incorporate the motif of lotuses into her works. She made teapot lids in the shape of lotus leaves, with a knob in the shape of a lotus flower. The lotus represented salvation even though—no, *because* it rose out of the mud. Making pottery was like that. Her works emerged from dirty clay to become teapots that helped slake people's thirst. What could be more miraculous?

However clumsily, Rengetsu worked hard at her pottery. She painstakingly fashioned veins in clay leaves and poked holes in the clay stems that formed handles. The veins she added with a prayer that salvation might extend to all people everywhere, the holes with the prayer that people's hearts might open to salvation.

Eventually her wares began to acquire a following. They were as ill-formed as ever, but something warm and friendly about them had an appeal. Now there was no end of buyers. Once their popularity caught on, they flew off the shelves. Merchants came to her now, wheedling for more. But Rengetsu worked alone, and there was a limit to what she could do. When merchants realized they couldn't keep her works in stock, they came up with the idea of selling fakes. In no time, five or six shops sprang up devoted to selling fake Rengetsu tea ware and vases. Friends of hers saw what was going on and hastened to warn her.

"Rengetsu! Something terrible is happening! The stores are full of forgeries of your work. Five or six places are selling them now."

Her response was strange. "Really? I'm glad people can make a living from the kind of pottery somebody like me makes." She smiled.

News of Rengetsu's tolerant reaction spread to her imitators, who faced a problem. Her teapots were decorated with poems of hers in her own writing, but the forgers, lacking education, couldn't replicate her calligraphy. Moreover, since they always used the same poems, people could easily tell their work was forged. They wanted to increase the number of poems they used, but coming up with proper thirty-one-syllable *waka* on their own was beyond them. Finally they went to see her with a peculiar request.

"Rengetsu, it's embarrassing to have to say this, but as you may know, we make copies of your *kibisho*. If we can, we want to expand our business. The trouble is, we can't imitate your handwriting. Could you help us?"

Again her response was extraordinary. "I see. Well, thank you for that. Working alone as I do, I can't increase my output, but never mind me. Go ahead and make all you can. I'll write the poems on them. Just bring whatever you make here and I'll take care of it." As they gaped, she added, "I'll give you each one of my teapots to take with you. You can copy it and then sell it. If you don't mix in something genuine once in a while, the imitations won't sell."

For over forty years, well into her eighties, Rengetsu continued to turn out Rengetsu-yaki, the name given to her pottery. Toward the end of her life she ordered clay from a man called Kuroda Kōryō, who also fired her works for her, and the Kuroda family is in possession of many letters from her. They reveal that when she was almost seventy she was making pottery at the rate of over one hundred pieces a month. That adds up to twelve hundred pieces a year, or well over fifty thousand in her lifetime. The population of Japan was then thirty-five million, with around seven million households. Nearly one in every hundred households across the country must have possessed at least one of her works. Taking into account the vast number of fake Rengetsu wares that were made, it's evident that her name must have been a household word all over Japan.

With fame came the annoyance of a stream of visitors. Her once-quiet retreat, set amid fields of radish and taro, became steadily noisier. She took to moving frequently. Having renounced the world as a Buddhist nun, she had almost no possessions to speak of. Apart from some rough tableware, she owned nothing but a potter's wheel and a writing desk, so all she needed was a big cart to pack up and move whenever she liked.

In the springtime she lived in Kita Shirakawa, where the cherry blossoms were beautiful, and in summer she sought the cool of the mountains near the great Buddha. In winter she would return to Okazaki and the vicinity of Chion'in. People called her "Rengetsu the house-hopper." She lived particularly often in the village of Shōgoin, located on what is now the campus of Kyoto University.

In the late twentieth century, Kyoto University Hospital set out to add an extension, an undertaking that required a preliminary archaeological survey since the university sits atop historic ruins. The area excavated to build a CT scan ward turned out to be one of Rengetsu's former homes, with scads of failed, unfired pieces of Rengetsu-yaki. The location corresponded to Rengetsu's address on old city maps, so researchers were able to confirm that she had lived there. The trove of unearthed pottery, indisputably her work, became an invaluable tool in distinguishing genuine Rengetsu-yaki from fakes. Since that discovery, digs have also been conducted at a number of similar sites in the same area, with her pottery turning up in at least three of them—an indication of how often she moved house in that area alone.

At some point a young boy came to live with Rengetsu in Shōgoin village. A shy boy from a neighboring house, at first he said nothing, but he seemed drawn to her pottery and was soon helping her transport clay. He was about thirteen or fourteen years old, the son of a dealer in religious robes with a shop at Sanjō Koromonodana. A childhood illness had left him deaf in one ear. His name was Yūsuke. He was to become the great calligrapher and painter Tomioka Tessai (1837–1924).

Rengetsu began to pour all her love and artistic sensibility on this boy. Yū-san, as she called him, was somehow under a shadow. It wasn't only that he was hard of hearing; there was more to it than that. He had no mother. For whatever reason, he lived alone with his father and, to Rengetsu's surprise, he always had his nose in a book. His father too seemed inordinately fond of reading; the two of them read constantly. The sight of the two males living alone and devoting all their time to books struck others as odd. From a distance the boy was charming, but seen close up he was badly cross-eyed. Whenever Rengetsu saw him, the word "pitiful" came to mind.

Eventually, after she got to know them better, she discovered why Yū-san—who turned out to be fifteen, older than he looked—was so downcast. The father had left his wife and older boy and come to the village with the younger son. Rengetsu found this strange. The father seemed amiable, not at all the type to cast aside his family business and his wife. "How did that come about?" she asked one day, and the father, casting a glance at his son, began a halting explanation.

"I'm solely to blame," he said. "It's all my fault that he's had to suffer."

"What do you mean?"

"For years my family has run a shop named Jūichiya that sells clerical robes and accessories. It's now in the seventh generation. But to my shame, I caused the family business to decline. My wife says it's because I was engrossed in books and neglected the shop, and she's probably right. I read so many books on Confucianism that people called me Bluebook." ("Bluebook" was the traditional term for a Confucianist, from the dark blue covers of the books they read.) "Then Yūsuke here was born. He was a pretty baby and his mother doted on him, but one day he developed a kind of rash all over his face. In hindsight, I should never have done it, but I wanted to make him better, so I rubbed ointment all over his face. That had a bad effect apparently, for when the rash was gone, so was his hearing. He can't hear at all in his right ear. If you speak in a loud voice into his left ear, he can just make out what you're saying."

"Oh, but he's a fine young man, isn't he? And reading books all the time is to his credit."

"Well, that's another story. Since he couldn't hear, he'd lose himself in books. He read so much, it was touching. But his mother said all that learning would get in the way of his running the shop, and when she caught him reading she'd scold him and threaten to take away his meals. She took his books and hid them. It broke my heart to see. And yet it was all my doing, every bit of it, since I ruined the family by reading so much in the first place. I couldn't argue with her. Instead I said, 'He's hard of hearing so he'll never be a shopkeeper anyway. Let's have him be a Shinto priest.' So we sent him to Rokusonnō Shrine on West Hachijō Street as an acolyte. Someone had said that if he was dressed up in a long-sleeved purple kimono with formal *hakama*, he'd make a grand-looking acolyte. But he was only eight years old. He must have been terribly homesick, sent away from his parents so young. When he finished his service there and came back, I left home with him. I wanted him to get a proper education."

Rengetsu looked at the youth. His eyes were so clear and pure that she could only wonder—could he really survive in a world so dark and sordid?

"I'm worried about his future," said his father. "How he'll get on in the world."

With good reason, she thought. Then she made a bold suggestion: "Could I ask to have him help me? As you can see, I am a potter, and I could use a strong pair of arms in my work."

"That would be wonderful! Let me ask him and see what he says." The father put his mouth close to the boy's left ear and said, "Would you like to be Rengetsu's helper?"

Instantly, the boy's eyes brightened.

From that day on, Yūsuke brought clay to Rengetsu, and when she had worked it and shaped it, he would load the wares in a cart and take them to Awataguchi kiln. It was backbreaking work, but he never complained. He stuck close to Rengetsu, as if seeking to fill the void left by his absent mother, and she returned his affection.

Yūsuke looked young for his age, but his extensive reading in the classics and his service as a shrine acolyte had given him a good grounding. When she talked to him about poetry or *The Tale of Genji*, he was always eager to hear more, and he had a quick mind. "Do whatever you want to do," she told him. "Meet the people you want to meet. See the sights you want to see, wherever that may take you."

When she realized he didn't have enough money for books, she gave him a generous share of her earnings and told him to use it for his education. When he objected, she said, "It's better not to keep money around the house. It's best if as much money leaves the house as comes into it."

Once he asked her, "Why are you so kind to me?" She answered lightly,

"I'm not being especially kind to you. I'm only trying in a small way to practice what's called 'equality of the self and others.' There's no difference between other people and oneself. That's what I believe." Then she laughed out loud. "Anyway, The best way to live in peace in this life is not to brood about things." Yūsuke felt sheepish at having brought it up, and never did so again.

However, when he caught a cold, she would look fierce and scold him: "Yū-san, you have to take care of yourself! You need to live a long life and serve society and others. Live quietly and patiently."

In 1853, they were astonished by the coming of Perry's Black Ships—a flotilla of American gunboats that marked an end to Japan's centuries of self-imposed isolation. The country entered a time of deep unrest. The most educated people in society went about with dagger eyes, calling loudly for the expulsion of foreign barbarians. Young Tessai, too, became excited and asked Rengetsu about the popular anti-foreign movement. Her response was unexpected.

"Yū-san, have Americans done anything bad to us? Why should we declare people who have never harmed us to be our enemies? That seems wrong to me. Having Americans here may turn out to be a refreshing change." Then she wrote out this poem:

> Along with spring rains
> Americans may come—
> May their presence
> Bring our land tranquility
> And refreshment.

Following the arrival of the Black Ships, everyone in Japan was up in arms, convinced that the Americans were bent on attack and must be driven away. People were swayed all in the same direction—a national trait of the Japanese, perhaps?—and virtually no one had the foresight to predict that the advent of

Americans might prove beneficial. It is something of a miracle that Rengetsu, knowing nothing of international relations, was able to come so easily to that conclusion.

Yūsuke came daily to Rengetsu's hut, and the two of them worked together from morning to night making pottery, like a true mother and son. In the course of time the shadow hanging over him vanished. Later, as Tomioka Tessai, he became recognized as the greatest artist in the literati painting tradition and a prodigious scholar schooled in Confucianism, Buddhism, Taoism, and Shintoism; in short, a man of letters whose like will not be seen again.

Rengetsu taught him many things, too. By this time famous, she was visited constantly by leading artists and literati of the day—all of whom she introduced to Tessai. Interestingly, she didn't treat him as a child. She spoke of him deferentially as "Tomioka Sensei," as if he were a distinguished master of the arts, and included him in their discussions.

Once again, Rengetsu began planning to move. Shōgoin village was near the city, so it was altogether too convenient. The number of people who came to see her morning and night troubled her—she could hardly get any work done. She longed to find a quiet mountain temple where she could live in peace. The next thing anyone knew, she was pushing a cart laden with her things.

With his connections, Tessai's father offered to help her find for a likely place. But despite her age (she was sixty-six, an old woman by any reckoning, though she looked twenty years younger) no temple was willing to take her in. Just as he was about to give up, he recalled a Sōtō Zen monk by the name of Hara Tanzan, the head of Shinshōji Temple in Kita Shirakawa village. Hara's temperament was free and easy; he was fearlessly outspoken, and later would be forced to leave Kyoto after openly berating the regent. This was just the man, Tessai's father decided, and asked him if he would be willing to rent a room to Rengetsu. "Certainly," came the unhesitating reply. "She can come tomorrow or whenever she likes."

Rengetsu was overjoyed. Shinshōji was the site of the grave of Ozawa Roan, that poet whom she so admired. She made up her mind: "I'll move tomorrow." A carpenter friend of hers named Matsubei made minor repairs on her new home every time she moved. According to his wife, Rengetsu sometimes moved as often as thirteen times in a year. "I can remember thirty-four of her moves in all," she said late in life. Of course, Rengetsu owned almost nothing. The only heavy things were her potter's wheel, a few pots and pans, and a small writing desk. Moving them wasn't hard, but she couldn't manage it alone. Tessai had hastily piled her things in the cart.

Tessai's father then did something admirable. He said into his son's good ear, "Go with her." From Shinshōji to the Awataguchi kiln was a distance of five miles, round trip. To go on making pottery, she would have to transport clay and works of pottery. "She can't do it alone," said Tessai's father. Tessai nodded in silent understanding. She was sixty-six, he twenty-one.

A strange living arrangement ensued, one that was to help form Tessai's character. Late in life, he would be known as an unworldly recluse. According to one source (*Geien issekiwa*, An Evening's Tales of Artists), Kyoto painters were by and large not of very good character. Most were happy to churn out work as long as they got paid in cash. But, "Though most literati are not indifferent to money and ugly rumors abound, Tessai, a man of pure and lofty character, stands alone among Kyoto *bunjin* as a shining example." Indeed, his refusal to paint for money was well known, although when struck by a friend's learning, he would take up his brush and produce a work that might have sold for millions, presenting it as a gift. His eccentricity was looked on with favor as the fruit of having spent his formative years at the side of the nun Rengetsu, and no doubt this was so.

By the Ansei era (1854–1860), Rengetsu's fame had spread throughout the land. Her pottery wares were in high demand. She was punctilious about some things, and kept a ledger marked "Accounts" in which she carefully noted all her financial dealings connected with pottery. Some people criticized this, saying it was inappropriate for a nun to keep accounts, but she paid no attention. Eventually, opinion swung her way. If other nuns did such a thing it would be vulgar, people decided, but in Rengetsu's case it had a certain charm. Her ledger became well known among her visitors.

Rengetsu obtained clay from the Awataguchi kiln and worked it every day. When she had made fifty or a hundred items, Tessai would cart them off to the kiln for her. She paid a fee of one silver coin when the quantity was low, twice that when it was high. She kept track of all sales in her ledger. She believed in providing for herself and not relying on charity, a conviction that never altered during her lifetime.

Yet when people asked her to write out a poem for them, as they often did, she never charged a fee: "An old nun like me may knead clay and sell earthenware, but refined taste is not for sale." At this time, Confucian scholars and poets commonly charged their pupils a registration fee. When they became famous enough, they would charge another fee to write or draw something on request. This was how they made a living, so by the standards of the day, for Rengetsu to decline a fee showed a lack of common sense.

Rengetsu also resisted publication of her poems. When a certain bookseller took note of her popularity and decided to issue a volume of her collected poems, she sent Tessai to talk him out of it. The bookseller was confused and angry. "Most poets would jump for joy at the mere sound of the word 'publish.' What's she got against it? We've already started printing. Who's going to cover our losses?"

This question left Tessai stumped. He consulted with Rengetsu, and to his surprise, she said, "I'll pay him for his losses. Go back and get him to call it off." But the bookseller held firm. Now Tessai got angry. "You've got no right to publish people's work without their permission in the first place. Twice now she's made it clear that she doesn't want the book published, and she's even offering to reimburse you for any losses you may have incurred. How can you possibly go on defying her?"

In the face of Tessai's wrath, the bookseller finally gave in. Tessai later said that this episode took all his negotiating skills. However, Rengetsu's refusal to allow publication of her poetry meant that works from her youth were lost. No one will ever be able to trace the arc of her life through her poetry, from her first wedding to her renunciation of the world.

Rengetsu's utter lack of desire for fame or money was remarkable. It was the same with her refusal to accept a fee for writing out poems. Word spread that as long as you paid for the paper, she would write all you wanted, and there were many takers. *Tanzaku,* the strips of fancy paper she wrote on, cost twelve mon per sheet, but she often gave away what she had written for free. Despite her love of quiet and privacy, when people came to see her she would welcome them in and, in exchange for their having come to see an old lady, press on them a poem written in calligraphy or a teapot.

She took pleasure in giving. One winter's day she set out for Kiyomizu Temple and along the way came across someone shivering in the cold. She took off her coat and gave it to him. Then when she arrived at the temple, on finding a drifter shivering in a thin kimono, she gave away her kimono. She went home wearing only an under-kimono, nose dripping.

Human beings were not the only objects of her generosity. People who ran into her on her walks often reported a strange scene. If she came across an ox or a horse by the side of the road, she would speak to it in coaxing tones, take a bit of rice-cake from her pocket, and drop it into the animal's feed-box. As the animal ate with relish, she would look on with pleasure, saying, "You work hard. You need to build up your strength." This was a form of entertainment for her.

When people chided her for throwing away good food by feeding it to horses, she calmly replied, "They're constantly overworked, the poor things. Look how big they are. They must get famished."

During the famine of 1850, when people lay dead in the streets, she sent for Tessai and handed him a large bundle of money with instructions to take it to Hiratsuka Hyōjūrō at the magistrate's office. Hiratsuka had the job of assisting the needy. Rengetsu had heard of this and wanted to contribute money for the purchase of rice to feed the starving. Tessai became concerned and asked how much was in the bundle. "Thirty ryo," she replied—the equivalent in today's money of nearly ten million yen (roughly US$100,000). She told him to deliver it anonymously and, reluctantly, he set off. But authorities, suspicious of the origin of this huge anonymous donation, interrogated him. Rengetsu's name soon came up. Apparently they realized that this gesture was something the unconventionally selfless nun might well do, and fortunately Tessai was released without further incident.

For the rest of his life, Tessai would wonder where such a huge sum of money could have come from. A penniless nun couldn't possibly have that kind of money. He told people she must have borrowed it from Daimaru or some other magnate she happened to know, but he was wrong. She had saved it little by little for a certain purpose: she wanted to build a bridge. This was her dream.

Around this time Rengetsu had moved back to Shōgoin village, which was near her birthplace, just across the Kamo River from Sanbongi. In the evening, the strains of the shamisen drifted over from the far bank, but there was no bridge. Marutamachi Street was cut off by the river, so that Sanbongi, on the far side, was near yet far. That was where her now-vanished parents had met. That knowledge may have contributed to her desire to build a bridge.

Marutamachi Bridge began to occupy her thoughts. In those days, the Kamo River ran in spidery streams in the dry riverbed, and people crossed over gingerly on planks. When the flow of water increased, the planks were soon swept away, and then anyone wishing to cross over had to go all the way to the bridge at Sanjō, a major inconvenience. When Rengetsu lived in Kawabata Marutamachi, near the river, she had all the more occasion to think about the need for a bridge, watching people cross with difficulty in hot weather and in cold.

For twenty years she had saved what little she could from making pots, but now it was to save precious lives that Tessai had carried the money to the government office. It took her another ten years to raise the money for the bridge. During that time, she kept on kneading clay, day after day after day. The bridge she finally built was just wide enough for carts to come and go, a ramshackle affair with low girders. But it did connect the banks of the Kamo River. She had made a bridge out of clay—the knowledge was deeply satisfying.

In the Bunkyū era (1861–1864), men of high purpose, known as *shishi* streamed to the capital from all over of Japan, bent on reforming the country by restoring power to the emperor and expelling foreign "barbarians." In response a band of masterless samurai formed the Shinsengumi, a pro-shogunate police force that strutted through the streets of Kyoto. At night there was mayhem: people being cut down, a man's bloody arm being thrown into someone's residence and the like. Rengetsu's house was frequented by leaders of the radical opposition to the shogunate. People began to warn her to be careful of the shogunate's spies. When Aizu forces entered the city and began attacking loyalist *shishi*, Tessai was also in danger, since he too had spoken out in favor of the imperial cause. After discussing it with Rengetsu, he decided to leave Kyoto for the time being and moved to Kyushu.

One night after he had left a strange incident took place. After Rengetsu had locked up and gone to bed, in the dead of night she heard a rattling at the door. The next thing she knew, a man was looming over her in the dark, demanding, "Hand over your money."

Rengetsu took it calmly. Without getting out of bed, she said, "Aren't you in the wrong house? Anyway, help yourself to anything you want." Then she got up and stirred the fire in the hibachi to brighten the room and help him search it. When he took all her kimono out of the closet and started to carry them off, she said, "Wait a minute. Wrap them in this." She held out a large *furoshiki* cloth. Then she said, "You must be hungry. Let me boil up some water and make you a nice bowl of hot tea-on-rice before you go."

"No time for that."

"Well, yesterday someone gave me some barley flour, so have that instead." She mixed the flour with warm water from the teakettle and made mush. He must have been starving. He gobbled up three bowlfuls and then rushed out without thanking her, no doubt feeling rather awkward.

In the morning, Rengetsu was woken by someone pounding on her door. "Rengetsu, something terrible has happened! A man carrying a big bundle of clothes collapsed and in the road. Your name was on the *furoshiki* he was carrying, so I came to tell you, figuring he must be someone you know."

"Well, I had a guest last night who said he needed money, so I gave him my kimono and a *furoshiki* to carry them in."

"You mean a thief. Come with me."

The dead man was indeed the thief of the night before. Rengetsu was horrified. The coroner determined that he had been poisoned. She was summoned repeatedly by the authorities. Where did she get the barley flour, they wanted to know. "I'm a nun living on my own," Rengetsu said. "Barley flour comes in handy, and I get it from various places. I can't remember where this batch came from."

They let it go. The case was never solved.

At first Rengetsu thought the thief might have taken his own life for some reason. However, various people told her in alarm that the stranger who had supplied the barley flour was a shogunate official. Rumor had it that Minister of the Center Sanjō Sanetsumu had been poisoned too, they said, and warned her to be careful.

Rengetsu understood the danger. She'd had close ties to loyalists like Yanagawa Seigan (1789–1858), who died just before the purge, and Umeda Umpin (1816–1859), a victim of the purge who died in prison. Shogunate critics like Kasuga Sen'an (1811–1878) and Tenshō, a monk of Kenninji Temple, still came calling. Despite herself, she became afraid.

"The world is in a dreadful state," she said. "Maybe it's all just a dream, but I can't help being frightened. I can't go to sleep without covering my chest with my arms."

"It's not safe. You'd better not receive any more guests."

She made a sign reading "Rengetsu is away" and hung it at her gate. But her house was tiny, barely three mats in size, and there was nowhere to hide. She lived behind a gardener named Uekichi, and asked his daughter to let on that she was away. Even so, people soon worked out that she was home and came in, saying "I don't mind if you're away." She was at a loss.

Thanks to Marutamachi Bridge, Rengetsu now lived half a mile or so from the Imperial Palace.

The chief priest of Jinkōin, a small temple across from Kamigamo Shrine to the north of the city, four miles from the Imperial Palace, told Rengetsu, "Living in Okazaki by Shōgoin as you do, I can't imagine why you would have so many callers, but if you really want to avoid them, why not move out this way?" Away from the bustling center of the capital, she could maintain her privacy and be out of danger.

Tessai quickly went off to see what could be done, asking the priest if he knew of any place in the area where Rengetsu might live.

"Hmm, no, nothing comes to mind."

"Then could she stay here in your temple?" Tessai asked.

"The teahouse is available…"

"That would do fine."

And so it was decided that she would move there. As usual, the move took little time. She had Matsubei the carpenter dismantle her small three-mat hut and rebuild it next to the teahouse, and soon moved in. The Jinkōin garden was beautiful. She enjoyed its quiet and serenity. This, she decided, was where she wanted to spend the rest of her life.

From then on, she stopped moving about, and this temple became her final dwelling-place. Her lifestyle remained as simple as before. She would work all day making pottery or doing other things, and at night she would light her lamp and recite the Mantra of Light. People who peeked in reported that she had fashioned little clay figurines of her parents and arranged them around a bowl she'd made, along with a little gold figurine of the bodhisattva Jizō, protector of those trapped in Hell. Every night she would make tea and pour it ceremoniously over them. After that she would spread out extremely plain bedding wrapped in rush matting and go to sleep.

Her diet, too, was simple, consisting of whatever the villagers gave her. She liked dining on discarded vegetable leaves, especially radish leaves. When farmers tried to give her vegetables, she would say, "Don't you have any radish leaves? That's my favorite." Then she would add with a laugh, "I may have been a chicken in a former life." When people offered her *takuan* pickles, she would smile and say, "Never mind the *takuan*. I'll just take the dried vegetables that stuck to the lid." Naturally, since she was a Buddhist nun, she ate no meat or fish, not even thin shavings of dried bonito. The only vegetables she wouldn't eat were oblong eggplants; the round variety she didn't mind. She explained her strange aversion this way: "Once I opened up the closet and found a dead rat whose blood had been sucked by a weasel. It looked exactly like a long eggplant. I can never forget the sight."

Rengetsu loved the village children. She kept writing paper on a shelf to give to them. They would come to her door and call, "Rengetsu, paper please!" She didn't mind in the least, and urged them to help themselves. Their parents took advantage of her generosity by sending them around whenever they ran out of paper. She understood this perfectly well but continued handing out free paper any way. In summer she made them each a belly-band boys and girls alike. Children in those days used to shed their clothes and run around in the buff, and she was determined to keep them from catching cold if she could, by keeping their bellies warm.

She cared very little about what she herself wore. Once when Tessai came over for a rare visit, he found her wearing a particularly gaudy kimono and commented on it. "Oh," she said, "do you think this is loud? I hadn't noticed. I just bought it because it was the cheapest, and it looked like it would wear well."

During the turbulent years leading up to the Meiji Restoration, Rengetsu lived peaceably in this country village. Her political sympathies, however, lay with Chōshū Domain. In 1863, when Satsuma and Aizu expelled seven lords of Chōshū from the capital, she made a point of going to see them off, filled with sadness and anger. Even so, she didn't share the views of the radical *shishi*, writing in a letter, "They've done terrible things, killing people in great numbers and displaying heads by the Kamo River. Now they've fled for other parts." She was adamantly opposed to killing.

Despite the remoteness of Rengetsu's hut, plenty of visitors found their way to her door. Leading artists of the day came to see her and chat, invariably bringing with them a painting or calligraphic work. She would paste the work to her wall and admire it for two or three days before taking it down to use as scrap paper, perhaps fastening it to a woven basket to make a lid for her hibachi. People told her this was a terrible waste, but she didn't listen. It wasn't that she had no appreciation for art, for in her alcove she displayed a painting of lotuses by Hine Taizan with an inscription by Hatta Tomonori. At one time she also had a drawing by Nukina Sūō, *Cascading Orchids and Bamboo*, but at some point it too disappeared. When asked what had happened to it, she said, "Someone wanted it, so I let them have it." That was her way; she would give away anything that someone asked for or admired.

Her utter unselfishness and indifference to worldly possessions were a continual source of amazement to others.

But she did seem to understand that paintings had monetary value. In 1866, the price of rice jumped due to the punitive Chōshū expedition and other events, and there was widespread poverty. At seventy-six, Rengetsu wrote out poems and painting inscriptions until her arms ached, donating the money she earned to charity and so putting food in the mouths of the starving. In fact, most of her extant works were written when she was seventy-six or seventy-seven.

The strife and bloodshed of the late Tokugawa era caused her anguish.

Whenever fighting broke out, she would pray continually that no one might be killed. When the second Chōshū expedition ended, she was elated and wrote to the scholar Murakami Tadamasa in Mikawa Province, "I understand that the punitive expeditions to Chōshū have stopped. I am very grateful that there is to be no more war. This is cause for celebration."

She was upset when fighting broke out between pro-imperial and Tokugawa shogunate forces at the battle of Toba-Fushimi. On January 3, 1868, the sound of gunfire could be heard all the way off in Jinkōin. Four days later, she wrote a letter to a distant relation in Tottori named Ōtagaki Yasohei: "War began in Fushimi on the night of the third day of the year, and yesterday the imperial forces won as far as Hashimoto, they say. Where will it all end? The chief priest at Ninnaji Temple, commander of the imperial army, raised the imperial standards, banners woven with the sun and the moon, and went as far as Tōji Temple. They say Satsuma troops led the way, bearing the flag of the rising sun, and everyone carried fans marked with the rising sun. Not knowing what the final outcome might be, I was afraid and went to the hills to hide in clumps of grass. I heard the rumors and made myself small, praying hard."

When word of the victory of imperial forces came, Rengetsu's face registered no joy. She received the news soberly. Told that the imperial army had won at Yawata, she asked anxiously, "What about the Tokugawa? Are they all right?"

"No," came the answer, "they're not. From Fushimi on, the ground is covered with the corpses of fallen soldiers. It's awful to see."

Rengetsu was rendered speechless; her eyes filled with tears. When she was alone, she wrote this poem:

As I listen
My tears wet my sleeve.
Bodies lying
Strewn in the streets—

Whose may they be?

Shortly after this, Rengetsu swung into action with a strength and determination amazing for a woman of her age. She started something extraordinary. She was determined to have talks with Saigō Takamori. The imperial army was dispatching a force to rout the remnants of the shogunate army. The Tokugawa were to be cut down as "traitors." But Rengetsu believed it was wrong for compatriots to be killing one another, and instinctively she felt that the best way to convince Saigō of this was through poetry. She put her whole heart into this poem:

> Friend or foe,
> Winner or loser,
> All arouse pity
> When one sees
> All are countrymen.

The words came naturally to her, and then she wrote them down and planned a meeting with Saigō. She had various connections. To begin with, she was acquainted with Kasuga Sen'an, his mentor. Hatta Tomonori and other poetry-loving samurai of Satsuma were constantly coming to see her. Even Tessai knew Saigō and had wrestled with him at the sumo wrestling dojo in Horikawa Hakatayama. Getting the poem into Saigō Takamori's hands would not be difficult.

In later years, some have claimed this episode never happened, that it is mere legend, but they are wrong. Saigō saw the *waka*. At a military conference in Ōtsu, he showed it to the generals, and their eyes were opened concerning the great civil war then brewing in the country. Saigō's philosophy had been "The country must be reduced to scorched earth; then we can build a new Japan." His encounter with Rengetsu changed him.

Today Saigō, Katsu Kaishū (1823–1899), and Yamaoka Tesshū (1836–1888) are given credit for avoiding an all-out attack on Edo Castle. But what really saved Edo from a sea of flames was the humane sensibility of the woman Rengetsu.

In the Meiji era, various distinguished persons came calling, wanting to see Rengetsu with their own eyes. Lord Maeda of Kaga came on horseback with a number of attendants. Lord Mōri of Chōshū also came. She treated them the same way she did everyone. "I'm so glad you came. Have a cup of tea before you go." She served not *matcha* from powdered green tea, as one would have expected, but ordinary tea from boiled tea leaves.

Lord Mōri was a man of strict principles, and the following day he sent a messenger with a message of thanks, a gold coin, and a sack of sugar. She expressed appreciation, but said, "For someone like me who has renounced the world, money is a hindrance, not a benefit. Please take it back." She did accept the sack of sugar, which she enjoyed sharing with the village children.

Once past the age of seventy, Rengetsu began to prepare for her death. She had a carpenter fashion her a typical cask-like coffin, which she used to store rice in. But time passed, and she didn't die. When someone poor in the village died, she would donate her rice-chest coffin. The villagers caught on, and when someone died, they would go to her for a coffin. Many a villager was buried in a coffin Rengetsu had intended for her own use. Each time, she would have a new one made. There is no telling how many coffins she ended up buying.

In her eighties Rengetsu grew frail, but when Tessai became a father, she rejoiced and made bedding for the infant out of a long under-kimono that had been her mother's. Then, without saying why, she asked Tessai to paint a lotus blossom and the moon on a large cotton cloth.

In 1875, at the end of October, she finally took to her bed with typhoid fever. November came and she was no better. At her request, they sent for Dr.

Andō Seiken, a specialist in Chinese medicine from her birthplace, Sanbongi. Unfortunately, even after he examined her, her condition didn't improve.

People encouraged her to be seen by a doctor of Western medicine. She actually was familiar with Western medicine and after the Restoration had sometimes been persuaded to try Western medications. "Your doctor's prescriptions are no good," people said. "Change to Western medicine." But she only shook her head slowly. "Life and death follow their own laws, they say. Please don't concern yourself about me."

In December, her breathing grew labored, and she made her last requests. "Put a dagger in my casket," she said. "Let no man touch my body." The words were solemn. She also asked that only Tessai be informed of her death, and others not be inconvenienced by news of her funeral.

She breathed her last at four in the afternoon on December 10, 1875. She left almost no possessions. All they found was a carefully folded white burial kimono and a white cotton cloth to lay over the coffin—the cloth that Tessai had decorated with a lotus and moon. When they spread it out, between the two images they found her death poem:

My one wish
For the afterworld
Is to sit upon a lotus flower
And gaze upon the moon
Unhindered by any clouds.

While to others the life of the nun Rengetsu may have seemed a thing of scarcely believable purity, she herself longed in the next life to have a heart as pure as the unclouded moon. People were moved by this discovery. Her neighbors in Nishi Kamo village mourned her especially. Every single person in the village came to her memorial service.

"How many coffins does this make now?" someone murmured, and as if that were a signal, they broke into sobs. One person who was present, Nishimura Yahei, later remarked, "Rengetsu was a living saint. When she died, my father and I attended her funeral on our knees. The cemetery was a few hundred yards from Jinkōin, and I will never forget that everyone in the village, young and old, wept aloud."

References

Kokudaya Jūzaburō

Anazawa, Yoshitarō, ed. *Taiwa-chō shi* [A history of Taiwa-chō]. Taiwa-chō, 1977.

Kokuonki in *Sendai sōsho Vol. 11*. Hōbundō Shuppan Hambai, 1972.

Yoshida, Katsuyoshi, ed. *Kokuonki oboe* [Notes on Kokuonki]. 2001.

Nakane Tōri

Inoue, Tetsujirō. *Nihon yōmeigakuha no tetsugaku* [The philosophy of Japanese Yangmingism]. Fuzambō, 1900.

Kumekawa, Shin'ya, ed. *Tōri ikō kai* [Annotated posthumous writings of Tōri]. Nakane Tōri ikō kankōkai, Chishōan-seki Hōryūji. Meiji Bunken, 1974.

Ōtagaki Rengetsu

Murakami, Sodō, ed. *Rengetsu-ni zenshū* [The collected works of the nun Rengetsu]. Rengetsu-ni zenshū hampukai, 1927.

Sugimoto, Hidetarō. *Ōtagaki Rengetsu*. Tōyō Shobō, Seigensha. 2004.

About the author

Michifumi Isoda

Born in 1970 in Okayama Prefecture, he is descended from a chief retainer of Kamogata Domain, a connection that led to an early interest in historical documents. In 2002, he received a Ph.D. in history from Keio University. Formerly on the faculty of Shizuoka University of Art and Culture, he is now an associate professor at the International Research Center for Japanese Studies in Kyoto. His bestselling novel *Bushi no kakeibo: Kaga-han gosanyōmono no bakumatsu ishin* (A samurai's account-book: The accounting officer of Kaga Domain on the eve of the Meiji Restoration) won the 2003 Shinchō Document Prize. Isoda has written many other works, including *Tensai kara Nihonshi o yominaosu* (Reexamining Japanese history through natural disasters) and *Tokugawa ga tsukutta senshinkoku Nihon* (The advanced nation of Japan that took shape in the Tokugawa era).

（英文版）無私の日本人
Unsung Heroes of Old Japan

2017年3月27日　第1刷発行

著　者　磯田道史
訳　者　ジュリエット・ウィンターズ・カーペンター
発行所　一般財団法人出版文化産業振興財団
〒101-0051 東京都千代田区神田神保町3-12-3
電話　03-5211-7282（代）
ホームページ　http://www.jpic.or.jp/

印刷・製本所　大日本印刷株式会社

© Michifumi Isoda, 2012
Printed in Japan.
ISBN 978-4-916055-76-7